The Hero
and
the Sea

Patterns of Chaos
in Ancient Myth

by Donald H. Mills

Bolchazy-Carducci Publishers, Inc.
Wauconda, Illinois USA

General Editor
Laurie Haight Keenan

Contributing Editor
James G. Keenan
D. Scott VanHorn

Cover Design
Adam Phillip Velez

Cover Illustration
Katsushika Hokusai
"The Hollow of the Deep Sea Wave off Kanagawa."
The Minneapolis Institute of Arts. Bequest of Richard P. Gale.

The Hero and the Sea:
Patterns of Chaos in Ancient Myth
Donald H. Mills

Published by
Bolchazy-Carducci Publishers, Inc.
1000 Brown Street
Wauconda, IL 60084 USA
www.bolchazy.com

Printed in the United States of America
2003
by United Graphics

ISBN 0-86516-508-4

Library of Congress Cataloging-in-Publication Data
Mills, Donald H., 1940-
  The hero and the sea : patterns of chaos in ancient myth / Donald H.
Mills.
    p. cm.
Includes bibliographical references and index.
  ISBN 0-86516-508-4 (pbk.)
  1. Epic poetry--History and criticism. 2. Poetry, Ancient--History
and criticism. 3. Bible. O.T. Genesis--Criticism, interpretation, etc.
4. Bible. O.T. Exodus--Criticism, interpretation, etc. 5. Heroes in
literature. 6. Sea in literature. 7. Heroes in the Bible. 8. Sea in
the Bible. I. Title.

PN1307 .M55 2002
809.1'3209352--dc21   2002153910

Contents

Foreword

Professor Mills here presents a work about a major mythic archetype, or mythologem, the struggle of the hero against the forces of chaos, especially watery ones, as incarnate in the stories of Gilgamesh, Achilles, Odysseus, and Jacob. But he extends the theme of watery chaos to examine heroic confrontations with chaos of many kinds. Detailed considerations of the four paradigmatic hero stories lie at the heart of the book.

Mills's study, virtually an extended essay, is initially framed by Eliade's well-known conception of myth as cosmic in its concerns and by the division of space (and time) into sacred and profane. The approach is grounded in an intelligent application of ritual theory, dominated by van Gennep's notion of liminality, later adopted and modified by Victor Turner. The study is marked by structural oppositions, principally between chaos and order. Since the author's approach is also functional (no surprise given the above), myth becomes a high stakes game: at issue are nothing less than the quest for a coherent view of the cosmos, and the viability and survival of myth-based communities.

In an unusual and moving Epilogue, Mills argues strongly for a correspondence between attempts to understand the universe through the modern science of chaotics and those that occupied the ancient mythmakers in the patterns they sought to discern and express in their concrete stories. The ancient patterns, therefore, are not really ancient, they are timeless and universal. Modern students of chaos sometimes use the same metaphor (water as chaos) as the ancient mythmakers, and they have, almost religiously, the very same aim: to seek and establish patterns of order within the seemingly random and chaotic.

At the outset, Mills clearly defines his essential working terms. The argument is always carefully expressed, easy to follow; the writing is seamless and unfailingly elegant. This seems a work produced by Mills's having taught the selected texts for many years, and from his having thought deeply about them with a thesis in mind. The learning is profound, but lightly worn: annotations and bibliography are fresh, but not overwhelming. This notwithstanding, experts can learn from this book, but so also under this design can undergraduates and the general public.

JAMES G. KEENAN
Loyola University Chicago

Preface

A number of ancient Near Eastern myths recount a hero's battle with a water demon or water divinity. These divinities often come to symbolize primordial or pre-cosmic chaos, and the hero's victory over his watery adversary is emblematic of a cosmic creation or re-creation. This study investigates how myths of heroic battle with chaotic adversaries inform and condition several ancient heroic narratives. In particular, it examines the ways in which this mythic pattern functions in response to the cultural needs, religious concerns, and worldview of its audience. The Babylonian hero Gilgamesh, the Greek heroes Achilles and Odysseus, and the Old Testament patriarch Jacob all encounter the chaotic in their respective struggles with watery adversaries.

It is the thesis of this study that these mythic narratives give vivid expression to the terrifying experience of the chaotic while providing the conceptual framework by which ancient poets could ritualize, in ways meaningful to their respective communities, the hero's movement from chaos to victory. Because myth and ritual each serve to make intelligible social organization and to clarify a multitude of problematic human relationships, the riddle of the chaotic lies behind every ancient mythmaker's struggle to express a sense of order in a world where chaos often seems to reign.

The last chapter explores points of contact between the ancient mythic patterns and the discoveries of modern scholars engaged in the theoretical study of chaos and chaotics.

There is, of course, much that could be written about the multicultural dimensions of the ancient Mediterranean civilizations and the interconnections of their world views, but I believe that *The Hero and the Sea* is unique in that it expands the realm of inquiry by using the methodological insights of literary scholars, comparative religionists, anthropologists and psychologists to explore ancient conceptions of chaos. For these ancient narratives of heroic struggle uniquely transcend time and culture to speak to the universal human condition. Thus, they give expression to all those hopes, aspirations, and fears that have defined, for ancient no less than modern thinkers, what it means to be human in a chaotic world.

I would like to express appreciation to the Department of Languages, Literatures, and Linguistics at Syracuse University for help with the some of the productions costs of this volume. I owe also a great debt of gratitude to those who have read the manuscript in whole or in part: Jim Bresnahan, Jeff Carnes, Laurie Winship, and the peer reader at Bolchazy-Carducci. Their efforts are deeply appreciated.

Finally, this book is dedicated to the memory of my parents, Naomi and Irvin Mills.

D.H.M.

Acknowledgements

The Greek font, *Milan Greek*, used in the quotations from the *Iliad* and the *Odyssey,* was developed by Ralph Hancock after a similar typeface used in an edition of Isocrates published in Milan in 1493.

The cover illustration is the wood cut titled "The Hollow of the Deep Sea Wave off Kanagawa" by Katsushika Hokusai (1760–1849), Japanese painter and wood engraver, born in Edo (now Tokyo). He is regarded one of the best representatives of the *Ukiyo-e*, or "pictures of the floating world" (everyday life), school of printmaking.

Used by permission of the Minneapolis Institute of Arts, a bequest of Richard P. Gale.

⚜
Chapter I
Mythic Patterns

Many ancient Near Eastern myths tell of a hero's battle with a water demon or water divinity. Such divinities often symbolize primordial or pre-cosmic chaos, and the hero's victory over his watery adversary is symbolic of a cosmic creation or re-creation.[1] There is, however, despite the consistency of its basic structure, a great deal of variety in the development, function, and meaning of this mythic pattern. This study investigates how myths of heroic battle with chaotic adversaries inform and condition several ancient heroic narratives. In particular, it examines the ways in which this mythic pattern functions in response to the cultural needs, religious concerns, and worldview of its audience.[2] By considering the commonalities of a mythic idea in different cultures and literary traditions, one can identify both convergences and differences, and gain thereby a fuller understanding of the unique interplay of differing mythic traditions in ancient Near Eastern and Greek thought.[3]

Although this study does not adhere to a specific methodology, nevertheless, in my attempts to understand this mythic pattern, I have found the writings of several structuralist and comparative theorists helpful, especially Arnold van Gennep's *Les Rites de Passage*[4] and Mircea Eliade's concept of *sacred space*,[5] both of which involve a number of useful cross-cultural and comparative observations.

The Nature of Myth

I understand myth as a traditional story that speaks to issues of great social and religious concern to mythmakers and their audiences. Both van Gennep and Eliade base their work on the perception that traditional societies uniformly posit a firm and clear distinction between the sacred and secular realms, or the *sacred* and *profane* in Eliade's terminology.[6] Because traditional societies perceive the relation between these two realms in ways that are doubtlessly determined by biological, environmental, and social experiences, such universal experiences provide the best explanation for those mythic and religious elements that transcend cultural, geographical, and political boundaries.[7]

In applying the concepts of *sacred and profane* to issues of mythic meaning, this study will take a broadly functional approach. By examining the specific mythic narrative, its time, place, and meaning, this study will ask how the narrative functions, not simply with respect to some known or unknown ritual, but in the broad cultural life of the mythmaker and his audience. To put it more directly: what did a particular myth or mythic pattern *mean* to those who *used* it? What religious, cosmological, or social concern did the myth address? What perennial terror of human existence did it seek to allay?

There are of course ritual dimensions to myth, just as mythic elements are often prominent in ritual. While much has been written in the ongoing myth-ritual debate, let it suffice at this point simply to note that myth and ritual share similar functional roles in the life of traditional societies.[8] In order to suggest the nature of this functional relationship I would first define myth as *an imaginative narrative dealing with cosmically significant acts of divine or superhuman beings.* By *cosmically significant* acts I mean those social or religious events that the mythmaker and his audience invest with transcendent meanings, thereby conceptualizing their relation to the world at large.[9] Ritual, moreover, when employed in concert with myth, is the means by which the community seeks to exercise some measure of control over those same cosmic events.

The rituals of traditional societies, then, provide the mechanisms by which the community seeks to renew its vitality and thus to insure its continuing viability. Carried out with regular frequency, and sanctioned by tradition, such rituals maintain the fundamental good will of the powers of the natural order toward the human community;[10] as such, these rituals and their proper observance are a matter of life and death both for the individual and for the community as a whole.

Simply put, traditional societies are naturally given to ritual and myth, two modes of activity by which they endeavor both to understand and manipulate the world around them. Thus mythic narrative and ritual performance each address the most essential needs, crises and dilemmas of primitive human existence, e.g. the production of food through the fertility of crops and domestic animals, the continuation of the community through marriage and procreation, and even the alleviation of the terror of death through funeral rites. Myth and ritual, moreover, often operate on metaphorical and symbolic levels. However, where myth employs verbal symbols, ritual uses symbolic objects and symbolic movement to achieve its ends. Yet, in spite of these differing symbolic modes, both serve to provide traditional societies with the means to address the perennial needs and crises of the community.[11]

This definition leads to several explicit propositions about the nature of myth and mythic narratives.

1. *Myths have an objective correlative.* In a mythic narrative, there is always an objective element, a fact, a situation, or some underlying reality, which the myth addresses and attempts somehow to explain. Paul Tillich once wrote: "Only when one's thinking has objective reference can a truly mythical element pulsate through it."[12] It follows that myth represents a reality with genuine cognitive status, and is open, therefore, to investigation with all of the tools available to literary and social scholarship.

2. *Myths are folk-creations.* They arise from the experiences and imaginations of common people; in general, they are *not* conscious inventions of self-conscious thinkers. (This distinction

would exclude, e.g., the *myths* of Plato or of the Manichaeans, whose fictions are elaborate, self-conscious, rational, and often unconvincing.) Rather myths are a cultural inheritance, a tradition handed down from one generation to another, and therefore invested with communal values. This explains the close association between a community and its mythology.

3. *Myths reflect social realities.* Because mythic narratives have their origins in the common life of a community, mythic stories tend to persist over time as a part of the community's traditional self-understanding. Often, for example, a myth encapsulates a community's sense of its identity, its concrete existence in time and place, and indeed is often a defining expression of its social vitality.[13] This is why traditional societies highly value their mythic traditions; they express something distinctive and meaningful about their existence as a community. Thus, myth comes to be an inseparable and indispensable part of the intellectual and spiritual life of traditional societies.

4. *Myths are transcultural.* Similar mythic ideas and patterns often appear in different cultural, geographic, and historical settings. A study that explores similarities in mythic narratives of diverse cultural origins needs to suggest, if only in a tentative and hypothetical way, explanations for such similarities. Parallels between Near Eastern and Greek myths are well known, and a number of competing theories have attempted to explain them. The simplest and most direct of these theories understand a process of diffusion, by which mythic ideas gradually spread through the Eastern Mediterranean in a form that was oral and piecemeal. In setting forth this theory Robert Mondi cautions against thinking of myths primarily as linear narrative accounts, but rather uses the phrase "conceptual foci" to suggest the mythic nuclei to which various ideas, images, and narrative motifs are attached.[14]

It is important to avoid the temptation of thinking in terms of a diffusion of literary, narrative, or textual materials, when in fact that which was diffused was probably non-narrative, that is to say, the inchoate themes, patterns, and general structures of thought that underlie both mythic and non-mythic conceptions. These patterns are marked by a fluidity, variability, and "protean process."[15] As a result, their actual formulation at any given time was determined by the mythmaker's individual touches as he tried to address the perceptions, expectations, and experiences of his audience. By their very nature, these metamythical elements are allusive and suggestive, existing separate from and outside of literary narratives. They are simply basic notions reflecting the principal assumptions about significant events in the life of a community.

A comparative approach, then, needs to be aware of such ideological structures and the conceptual relationships latent in mythic narratives. Not only must it be clear about the fact of non-narrative diffusion of mythic ideas, it also needs to consider the extensive nexus of mythic themes common to Near Eastern and Greek thought.

In considering mythic ideas expressed in literary and narrative settings, it is also important to keep in mind the distinction between the mythic idea itself and its actualization in a poetic narrative. Mondi has well expressed the dangers the failure to observe this distinction entails:

> One problem that frequently bedevils interpretation is that the texts often presuppose and exploit a popular tradition of mythic ideas, a latent substratum never overtly actualized in the surface narrative. Each literary work has its own unique program, and this thematic overlay often conceals from us the very mythic associations upon which it depends for its meaning and force— particularly in those cases where tension is generated by divergence from an audience expectation based on this underlying tradition. The comparison of conceptual motifs,

more so than that of narrative parallels, can provide
access to this hidden world of shared mythic thought.[16]

A useful term for such a latent pattern is *mythologem*, which I
understand to be *a perduring mythic theme recurring in various
narratives, which has an implicit conceptual consistency*. Since it
is by nature a kind of archetype,[17] *mythologem* is a primal paradigm, a pattern that goes back to the beginnings of things, expressing the perennially recurring experiences of the human species. It
also conveys what is *true* for every individual (since it is connected
to his or her personal experiences); at the same time, it is also a
collective statement of the essential nature of life for every individual who ever lived.[18]   Although a mythologem tends to be
relatively stable, it lacks the richness of imagination and drama
that a particular storyteller can bring to his narrative; all the same,
it contains within it the conceptual core, the seed, as it were, with
the potential to grow into the full expression of that which has
abiding interest for the human community and its traditions.[19]

It is also important to note that a mythologem is analogical:
like a simile or metaphor, it often has a non-literal and altered
sense of meaning. For example, Homer's mythic proposition that
"Okeanos is the father of all" contains an implicit analogy compar-
ing the sea's procreative functions to those of a father. Further,
because a mythologem often has a paradigmatic dimension, it is
also extensible; that is, it may expand to include other mythic and
non-mythic conceptions. For example, the Old Testament writers
expanded the mythologem of cosmic order from primal chaos to
include the idea that chaos returned with the flood; ultimately this
expanded mythic pattern became a central element in the Israelites' historical self-understanding.[20]   A mythologem, therefore,
like mythic narrative itself, offers the means by which to order
experience and interpret the world. As such, it contributes to a
systematic and coherent worldview, which can be critically studied, analyzed, and interpreted.[21]

There is, moreover, a non-cognitive element in myth. Mythic narratives often give expression to the fears, hopes, aspirations, and dreams of individuals and communities. Such myths evoke emotional and valuational responses, which need to be addressed to understand fully the nature and meaning of the mythic narrative. For example, a complete understanding of the Oedipus myth must address the non-cognitive and affective dimensions of the incest taboo.

The Nature of Ritual

Turning to ritual, I define it as a *predictable pattern of activity, sanctioned and maintained by tradition, and regularly repeated by a community, which has certain expectations regarding its meaning and efficacy.* Ritual behavior is primarily communal, that is, every ritual is a social act; it arises from interactions among the members of a community and defines their roles in the community as a whole. As Walter Burkert writes: "ritual creates and affirms social interaction."[22]

Ritual is also the community's expression of its relation to external powers and entities. Irrespective of whether the external comprises other communities, or the unseen elemental powers of nature, ritual provides the means by which the community seeks to confront the *other* as efficaciously as possible. Thus understood, ritual is perhaps the most elemental way in which traditional societies deal with the chaos of the world.[23] It is a community's attempt, through regularized, stereotypical, and measured acts, to create order in a disorderly and unpredictable world.

As the community struggles to define itself and give meaning to its existence over and against the world *out there*, it finds it necessary to include some individuals, and to exclude others. Some who were once included are excluded, and some, once excluded, are brought back into the social circle, often with changed status. This communal behavior very likely goes back to Paleolithic times when the bonding of hunter groups necessarily determined the success of the hunting party. It is not difficult to imagine how patterns of grouping and bonding became ritualized, ultimately outliving the immediate needs that brought them into existence.[24]

Arnold van Gennep was the first to recognize and describe the three-fold nature of bonding and incorporation rituals. Relying on his analysis of *Rites of Passage*,[25] he came to see that the *raison d'être* of all rituals was the transformation of social status: ritual provides the means by which the community protects the transitions from one stage of life to another, since such transitions are always felt to be fraught with danger and crisis. Underlying this sense of crisis is the almost universal conception in traditional societies of a clear line of demarcation between the sacred and the secular. Implicit in this conceptual division is also the sense that there is an ongoing, dynamic interrelationship between human social and biological life and the cycles of the cosmos.[26] The three stages, then, in all *Rites of Passage* consist of the old status, the new status, and the in-between stage, a kind of limbo, or no-man's land, to which van Gennep applied the Latin word for 'threshold', *limen*. This *liminal* stage represents the undefined, the chaotic, through which every ritual subject or initiand must pass on the way from the old to the new. It is reasonable to expect, therefore, that mythic narratives of heroic struggle with the chaotic will exhibit characteristics of the liminal stage in ritual passage.

It follows, then, that all rituals of transition function within the larger context of social dynamics. As real events in the experiences of a community, rituals bear upon all the other elements of a people's cultural life: its literature, myth, history no less than the individual and collective life experiences of its members are all touched by ritual. Rituals of transition also facilitate role-assumption in a typical life span; that is, they aid in defining social roles for individuals at various points in their lives. Finally, transition rituals serve to free both individuals and the community from affective anxieties. This is ritual's non-cognitive role of alleviating human terror in the face of a seemingly arbitrary and hostile cosmos.[27]

Van Gennep's important contribution, therefore, lies in his providing sociologists and anthropologists with a methodology for analyzing the functional role of ritual as a social phenomenon.[28] Because mythic narratives also reflect social realities, van Gennep's ritual categories for social change are applicable to the analysis of mythic narratives. For these categories reveal the all but universal patterns of thought and action by which traditional societies attempt to create a sense of order at just those times of social crisis when the terrifying powers of the chaotic threatens to break through and destroy the very fabric of human community. Accordingly, rituals of passage bear upon mythic stories of chaos and conflict precisely because they occur in contexts of crisis. The mythic idea of heroic conflict with watery chaos seems the symbolic expression of the desire to negate mythically and ritually the perils of social transition and cosmic change.

The well-known anthropologist, Victor Turner, took up van Gennep's premises, but argued that rituals stand over and against social structures, confronting them in an on-going process of change. For this reason the confrontational aspect of ritual vis-à-vis social structure is for him its most significant element; the liminal stage of the *ritual process* is not merely one of three ritual stages, but rather the essential element that defines the ritual as a whole. Standing in opposition to the structures and behaviors of quotidian life, the entire ritual is *liminal*. Turner sees ritual as a kind of counter-structure to the normative social structures of everyday communal life. Thus, he emphasizes the ambiguous nature of ritual subjects in their liminal passage. Their liminal position is unstable in relation to the stability of both their past and future status. This social ambiguity is expressed by a rich variety of symbols: death, being in the womb, invisibility, darkness, bisexuality, wilderness, an eclipse of sun or moon all express the indeterminate and ambiguous nature of liminality.[29]

While there is much to recommend Turner's interpretation of van Gennep's *Rites de Passage*, I believe that his views are open to the criticism of over-emphasis on the *antistructural* role of ritual in the dynamics of social change. By stressing liminality, he minimizes the importance of van Gennep's other two ritual stages. To be sure, liminality is important, but it also necessarily follows from the ritual stage of separation and leads to social reincorporation. Further, one ought not overlook the fact that social order and ritual often play reciprocally supportive roles—for ritual often is the means by which a community reincorporates those whom it has excluded for a time and for a purpose. To put it even more strongly, rituals of liminality often sanction forms of behavior *that are required* by the social structure. One thinks of induction ceremonies as the ritual means by which, e.g., new military recruits are not only given license to use normally unsanctioned violence, but also inducted into a society that has made such license the basis for its required code of behavior.

Nevertheless, Turner's argument posits two major models for human interrelatedness, one marked by a structured, differentiated, and often hierarchical system of political-legal-economic positions, and the other an unstructured, relatively undifferentiated community of equals, which he connects to the liminal stage of *Rites de Passage*.[30] Turner employs the Latin term *communitas* to describe this model of an unstructured community of equals and the relationships that naturally develop because of their shared liminality. *Communitas* arises from the fundamental human need for a sense of connectedness, which the hierarchical structures of society tend to repress; this need, moreover, expresses itself in religious rituals and indeed is their very *raison d'être.* Using this distinction between social structure and *communitas*, Turner argues that social life for individuals and groups is a type of dialectical process involving movement back and forth "through a limbo of statuslessness."[31] Because he emphasizes the liminal as the determining element in all ritual, Turner tends to downplay the role of hierarchy in establishing and promoting social order. Consequently, he minimizes this aspect of ritual. It seems relevant to note, however, that ritual is often the very means by which those who have something at stake in maintaining the structures of social organization maintain both social order and their own place in it.[32]

The importance of Turner's analysis for this study lies in the underlying pattern of dialectical movement into and out of liminality. Ancient stories of heroic conflict with watery chaos involve significant changes in the hero's social orientation and connections. Moreover, those changes are patterned, as will be seen in the following chapters, on ritual movement into and out of liminality. Although the heroic struggle with the chaotic is often solitary and individual, the ancient storytellers invested their tales, either consciously or unconsciously, with far-reaching societal implications. For such liminal movement is motivated by the attempt of traditional societies to confront the chaotic in their natural and social realms. Because Turner sees only two modalities and defines them in terms of one another, to wit, "*communitas* emerges where social structure is not,"[33] they seem to represent an even more basic pattern: order and chaos. This means, then, that the sense of interdependence, of egalitarian mutuality in *communitas* is in fact the positive antithesis of chaos: it facilitates human bonding and human community just at those times of social crisis when unity of purpose is most needed.

The *Sacred Center*

Like Turner, Mircea Eliade, the prolific scholar of comparative religions, also takes a functional approach to myth. For him myth and ritual are the means by which traditional societies recall the primordial time when gods or superhuman heroes took the paradigmatic first steps that established all subsequent patterns of meaningful human activity. This primordial *once upon a time* is marked in primitive thought by the irruption of the sacred into the profane; taking place in the time of the *ancestors,* such prototypical theophanies and hierophanies are recalled and repeated by ritual acts and by the retelling of mythic narratives. By thus *recalling* and reexperiencing the salvific powers of the mythic past, traditional societies confront present crises. In this way, myth and ritual perform a restorative function; by calling into play perduring cosmic forces, they correct the ephemeral dislocations and imbalances of the present.

Another useful concept Eliade brings to his study of myth and ritual is that of the *sacred center.* In addition to the pervasive dichotomy of *sacred and profane*, traditional societies conceive their world as a microcosm. Beyond the boundaries of the closed and finite world of human experience lies the domain of the unknown, the formless, the chaotic. It is the realm of death, destruction, demons, and monsters. On this side there is ordered space, the realm in which we live and experience the orderliness of the familiar and known. Thus, the antithesis of *sacred and profane* becomes also the opposition of two antithetical realms of being, one marked by predictability, familiarity, and order, the other by disorder, strangeness, and chaos.

Every place, moreover, in which humans live, every inhabited region has a sacred center, that is, a place that is sacred above all others. This is the unique and special realm where the sacred manifests itself in its totality through theophanies and hierophanies. This space is marked by having an essential reality, for only the sacred is real. It is real precisely in the sense that in such space one has direct contact with the *sacred*.34 These sacred spaces are often symbolized and embodied by holy places of every kind: temples, mountains, and even cities. In short, every place where the sacred bursts through into the profane becomes a sacred center. The affective consequences of this attitude—for it is more than a philosophic theory, a religious disposition, or cultural *Weltanschauung*—is a desire, indeed a deeply felt yearning to move toward the center, because only there can one find "integral reality—sacredness." In fact, Eliade goes on to observe: "man can live only in a sacred space, in the 'Centre'." This strange unspoken aspiration he connects with the wish to transcend the human condition, and somehow to recover the primordial state of divinity. This means, then, that the sacred center is a source of immortality, both for the cosmos itself as well as for individual human beings. To quote him in full:

> [There is] at least one neglected aspect of the symbolism
> of the Centre: that there is not only an intimate inter-
> connection between the universal life and the salvation
> of man, but that it is enough only to raise the question of
> salvation, to pose the central problem; that is, the prob-
> lem—for the life of the cosmos to be forever renewed.
> For...death is often only the result of our indifference to
> immortality.35

Eliade's work is useful for this study in that, by showing the sacred as the realm of life and order, and the profane as the realm of death and chaos, he has demonstrated the pervasive presence of the chaotic in mythic thought. The almost universal human impulse to enter the realm of the sacred through myth and ritual expresses the desire to transcend the chaotic realm of quotidian existence, to leave behind the ambiguities of the human condition, and to aspire to divinity. This is the emotive appeal in stories of the mythic warrior confronting watery chaos. In its attempt to participate in his victory, the community appropriates his intuited movement from the profane to the sacred realm. Thus, the dichotomy of *sacred and profane* as mutually exclusive realms, and the recalling of primordial sacred time through myth and ritual, are two manifestations of the desire to move beyond the unpredictable and chaotic; only here lies the hope of release from ultimate chaos and the acquisition of immortality.

The premise of this study, then, is that a functionalistic approach to the interpretation of myth and ritual can help elucidate the meaning of mythic patterns in heroic narratives. I find myself in warm sympathy with the oft-quoted functionalist proclamation of Malinowski:

> Studied alive, myth, as we shall see, is not symbolic, but a direct expression of its subject matter; it is not an explanation in satisfaction of a scientific interest, but a narrative resurrection of a primitive reality, told in satisfaction of deep religious wants, moral cravings, social submissions, assertions, even practical requirements. Myth fulfills in primitive culture an indispensable function: it expresses, enhances, and codifies belief; it safeguards and enforces morality; it vouches for the efficiency of ritual and contains practical rules for the guidance of man. Myth is thus a vital ingredient of human civilization; it is not an idle tale, but a hard-worked active force; it is not an intellectual explanation or an artistic imagery, but a pragmatic charter of primitive faith and moral wisdom.[36]

Heroic Encounters with the Chaotic

The focus of this study, then, will be the mythologem of heroic battle with the chaotic as it recurs in several ancient mythological traditions. The working hypothesis of this study is that while the battle with the chaotic takes different forms and different conceptualizations, the underlying pattern remains conceptually consistent. Using the approach of van Gennep and Turner, specifically that liminality is the expression of the chaotic, and Eliade's notion that the profane is the realm of the chaotic as opposed to the sacred, this study takes as its premise the proposition that the dichotomy of order and chaos underlies every mythic tale of heroic battle with the chaotic.

In the following chapters, we shall see how the hero of the *Gilgamesh Epic* confronts the chaotic, first in the person of Enkidu, then in the conflict with the monster Huwawa and the Bull from Heaven, and finally in his inner spiritual struggle with death, which is expressed symbolically through the story of Utnapishtim and the flood. In the *Iliad,* Achilles confronts the chaotic in his battle with the Scamander River. For Odysseus, the battle with the chaotic comes in his encounter with an angry Poseidon, his shipwreck, and, in subtle and far-reaching ways, through his encounter with Calypso. In the Old Testament, the patriarch Jacob meets potential annihilation at the river Jabbok, when he wrestles with God.

What then do all of these mythic encounters have in common?

1) A physical battle with an adversary who comes to symbolize the chaotic.

2) A struggle that occurs in the realm of the liminal, which means that the conflict has both psychological and social implications.

3) A religious dimension in the conflict that finds expression through the polarities of *sacred and profane* because, like liminality, it addresses perennial crises of human existence.

All of these mythic narratives endeavor on the one hand to give meaning to the terrifying experience of the chaotic while on the other to provide the underlying conceptual framework by which to ritualize, in ways meaningful to the life of their respective communities, the heroic victory over the chaotic. I would also make the bold claim that, because myth and ritual each serve the functional end of making intelligible social organization and of clarifying a multitude of problematic human relationships, the riddle of the chaotic lies behind every ancient mythmaker's struggle to express a sense of order in a world where the chaotic often seems to reign.

Finally, the last chapter will explore points of contact between the ancient mythic patterns and the discoveries of modern scholars engaged in the theoretical study of chaos and chaotics.

Notes to Chapter I

[1] The earliest example of this mythic pattern is the Babylonian epic of creation, *Enûma Elish*. It relates how Marduk, the principal divinity of Babylon, engaged Tiamat in battle, and having defeated this goddess of the chaotic sea, used her body to create the universe.

[2] Clyde Kluckhohn observes, "The structure of new cultural forms (whether myths or rituals) will undoubtedly be conditioned by the pre-existent cultural matrix. But the rise of new cultural forms will almost always be determined by factors external to that culture: pressure from other societies, biological events such as epidemics, or changes in the physical environment." Clyde Kluckhohn, "Myths and Rituals: A general theory," originally published in *Harvard Theological Review* 35 (1942), 45–79, and republished in Robert A. Segal, *The Myth and Ritual Theory*, (Malden, MA: Blackwell Publishers Ltd., 1998), 313–340.

[3] Considerable debate on the question of Near Eastern influence on the origins and development of Greek civilization has been occasioned by Martin Bernal's controversial book, *Black Athena: the Afroasiatic Roots of Classical Civilization*, Vol. I (New Brunswick, NJ: Rutgers University Press, 1987). This study will not contribute to that debate except tangentially. I take it as a given that Hellenic civilization, from Mycenaean times into the historical period, was influenced by its various neighbors around the eastern margin of the Mediterranean. Cf. T.B.L. Webster, "Eastern Poetry and Mycenaean Poetry," in his *From Mycenae to Homer*, (London, 1958). The intensity of that influence, and the degree to which the scholarly literature has accurately understood and reported it, I leave to others to assess.

[4] Arnold van Gennep, *Les Rites de Passage* (Paris: Emile Nourry, 1909, reprinted by Johnson Reprint Corporation, New York: 1969). Translated as *The Rites of Passage* by Monika Vizedom and Gabrielle Caffee (Chicago: University of Chicago Press, 1960). All English citations of van Gennep are from this translation.

[5] Mircea Eliade, *Images and Symbols, Studies in Religious Symbolism*, translated by Philip Mairet. (New York: Sheed and Ward, 1969).

[6] Monika Vizedom, Rites and Relationships: Rites of Passage and Contemporary Anthropology (Beverly Hills, CA.: Sage Publications, 1976), 6.

7 To make a similar point, Arnold Toynbee (in his *A Study of History,* abridgment of vols. I–VI [New York: Oxford University Press, 1946] 41) quotes J. Murphy's *Man: His Essential Quest,* 8–9: "The resemblances in man's ideas and practices are chiefly traceable to the similarity in structure of the human brain everywhere, and in the consequent nature of his mind. As the physical organ is, at all known stages of man's history, substantially the same in constitution and nervous practices, so the mind has certain universal characteristics, powers and methods of action ..."

8 Kluckhohn, *op. cit.* (340), argues that myth and ritual tend to be universally associated because they have a common psychological basis and that both address fundamental "needs" of the society.

9 In a similar vein, Albert Lord defines myth as "a traditional narrative in the 'sacred' realm, a story springing from the needs of both individual and community, which is believed in and has a serious function." (Albert B. Lord, "The Mythic Component in oral Traditional Epic: its Origins and Significance," in W. M. Aycock and T. M. Klein, *Classical Mythology in Twentieth-Century Thought and Literature* [Lubbock, TX: Tech Press, 1978], 145–161.)

10 Lauri Honko defines ritual as "traditional, prescribed communication with the sacred." "Theories Concerning the Ritual Process: An Orientation," in Honko, Lauri, ed. *Science of Religion, Studies in Methodology: Proceedings of the Study Conference of the International Association for the History of Religions* (The Hague: Mouton Publishers, 1979), 373.

11 Cf. H. S. Versnel, "What's Sauce for the Goose is Sauce for the Gander: Myth and Ritual, Old and New," in Lowell Edmunds, *Approaches to Greek Myth* (Baltimore: Johns Hopkins University Press, 1990), 58.

12 "The Religious Symbol," *Daedalus* (1958), 21.

13 For an interesting discussion of one example of this phenomenon cf. P. Vidal-Naquet, "The Black Hunter and the Origin of the Athenian Ephebia" in The *Black Hunter: Forms of Thought and Forms of Society in the Greek World*, 106–28. Tr. A. Szegedy-Maszak (Baltimore, 1986).

14 Robert Mondi, "Greek Mythic Thought in the Light of the Near East" in Edmunds, *op. cit.* (note 11 above), 145.

[15] This expression is used by John B. Vickery, *Myths and Texts: Strategies of Incorporation and Displacement* (Baton Rouge: Louisiana State University Press, 1983), 2.

[16] Mondi, *Greek Mythic Thought* (note 14 above), 146–47.

[17] I do not mean by this to equate mythologem with Jung's archetype; nor do I take it to mean *structure* as Levi-Strauss has employed this term. My reason for making these distinctions is the conviction that mythologem should not be given a privileged ontological status. Rather a mythologem comes into existence simply as an expression of common, universal social situations. For example, a "mother figure" in a myth or ritual does not have a metaphysical reality apart from the simple fact that every human being has a mother. The "mother figure" in myth, then, is merely the verbalization of a mythmaker's reflection on this universal biological relationship. Cf. Versnel's discussion of sociobiology in Edmunds, *op. cit.* (note 11 above), 61.

[18] This applies of course only to genuine mythic ideas; excluded are those mythic expressions that are so transcendent as to be meaningless for the conditional here and now, or so individual and solitary as to be only solipsistically meaningful.

[19] Cf. Vickery, *Myths and Texts* (note 15 above), 28.

[20] See the discussion in Chapter Five, *infra*.

[21] For this discussion of mythologem and mythic structure I am indebted to the persuasive discussion of models in Ian G. Barbour, *Myths, Models, and Paradigms: A Comparative Study in Science and Religion* (New York: Harper & Row, 1974).

[22] Walter Burkert, *Homo Necans: The Anthropology of Ancient Greek Sacrificial Ritual and Myth* (Berkeley: University of California Press, 1983), 23.

[23] Cf. H. S. Versnel, "What's Sauce for the Goose" (note 8 above), 64: "the most elementary and primordial scheme of (originally biosociological) functions has been conserved and transformed, in ritualized and mythicized form, at precisely those points where human society still experiences primal crises most intensely."

24 For an interesting and provocative discussion of this process, see Walter Burkert's chapter, "The Evolutionary Explanation: Primitive Man as Hunter" in *Homo Necans* (note 22 above).

25 Arnold van Gennep, *Les Rites de Passage* (note 4 above, 1969 ed.)

26 Monika Vizedom, *Rites and Relationships* (note 6 above), 6.

27 For this threefold understanding of ritual functions, I am indebted to Monika Vizedom's discussion in *Rites and Relationships* (note 6 above), 24.

28 For a good, concise description of the influence and developments of van Gennep's theory of ritual passage by subsequent scholars, the reader is referred to Lauri Honko, *Ritual Process* (note 10 above), 369–72.

29 Victor W. Turner, *The Ritual Process, Structure and Anti-Structure* (Chicago: Aldine Publishing Company, 1969), 95.

30 Turner, *ibid.*, 96.

31 Turner, *ibid.*, 97.

32 For similar reasons, Lauri Honko is likewise not persuaded of the importance of Turner's *communitas* in rituals of passage, cf. *Ritual Process* (note 10 above), 386.

33 Turner, *The Ritual Process* (note 29 above), 126.

34 Mircea Eliade, *Images and Symbols* (note 5 above), 40.

35 Mircea Eliade, *Images and Symbols* (note 5 above), 56.

36 Bronislaw Malinowski, *Myth in Primitive Psychology* (*The Frazer Lectures,* New York: W.W. Norton, 1926), 73. I find it most telling that, in quoting this famous passage, Eliade leaves out the words: "is not symbolic, but a direct expression of its subject matter": Mircea Eliade, *Myth and Reality* (New York: Harper & Row, 1963), 20. Although the myths of Malinowski's Trobriand Islanders may not be "symbolic" and direct, this is certainly not true of other mythologies.

Chapter II

Gilgamesh and the Heroic Confrontation with Death

The *Gilgamesh Epic* is one of the world's first great pieces of epic literature; it is a heroic story whose unique humanism transcends limits of time, location, and culture. The influence of the poem was wide and deep; not only did it color all subsequent Near Eastern literature, it has also left traces of its influence in Greek and Roman literature as well.[1] Its existence in the Sumerian, Old Babylonian, Akkadian, Hittite, and Hurrian languages indicates its widespread popularity. Near Eastern scholars are in general agreement that the story of Gilgamesh originated as a Sumerian epic, although its Babylonian version is the best attested and most complete. Its hero was a historical figure, a king of the Sumerian city of Uruk (also called Erech), who lived in the first half of the third millennium (ca. 2600) BCE. The date of the poem's composition may have been as early as 2,000 BCE, but its fullest surviving version originated in the royal library of Ashurbanipal at Nineveh, dating from the seventh century BCE.

The themes and concerns of the *Gilgamesh Epic* make clear its profoundly mythic scope and attitude, and, as will be seen, it shares a number of mythic conventions and conceptions with the literatures of other mythopoetic peoples.[2]

The epic opens with the hero Gilgamesh reigning over the city of Uruk. His behavior is carefree, extroverted, unrestrained, and autocratic—behavior best characterized as child-like and irresponsible: he sleeps with the city's wives and the pretty girls, and compels the young men to corvée duty. The people of Uruk pray for relief from his depredations, and in answer to their prayers, the gods create Enkidu. Described as a wild man, Enkidu has a body completely covered in hair; he feeds on the grass of the fields with the gazelles, and drinks with them at their watering holes. When

Gilgamesh learns of his existence, he sends a sacred prostitute to ensnare this wild man of the steppes. When she displays her considerable sexual charms, desire overwhelms Enkidu. For six days and seven nights, he makes love to her. Upon his return to the animals, they flee; he has become, however, so enervated and weak that he can no longer keep up with them.

In order to compensate him for his loss of physical vigor, the prostitute bestows upon Enkidu the gifts of human wisdom and civilization: providing him with clothing, she introduces him to the shepherds, and teaches him the use of solid food and strong drink in place of the milk of wild animals. Making his way to the royal city of Uruk, Enkidu learns of Gilgamesh's uncouth behavior and is deeply offended. Intercepting the king on his way to a tryst, he engages the king in a wrestling match; Gilgamesh eventually gains the upper hand, Enkidu recognizes him as a true king, and they become inseparable friends.

The first adventure of this heroic duo involves a journey to the cedar-forest where they purpose to kill the giant Huwawa (Assyrian Humbaba), in order for Gilgamesh, according to the Babylonian version, to make a name for himself and win glory. In spite of initial setbacks, they defeat Huwawa. At first, Gilgamesh is inclined to heed the monster's pleas for mercy and to accept his offer to become his servant, but Enkidu counsels firmness, and the two heroes dispatch their victim.

In the poem's next episode, Gilgamesh has bathed and adorned himself royally when Ishtar, the goddess of love, offers him the opportunity to become her husband. He rejects her advances with more insolence than tact, listing the fates of her previous lovers: Tammuz she turned into a bird; the lion was thrown into a pit, etc. Because of this rejection, the goddess rushes off to her father, Anu, and demands that he create the Bull of Heaven to avenge this slight to her godly dignity. The two heroes, however, are able to dispatch this second monster as easily as the first.

Although the Bull of Heaven turns out to be no real threat to the heroes, the encounter proves to be the undoing of Enkidu. When Anu demands the death of either Gilgamesh or Enkidu as punishment for slaying the Bull of Heaven, and a council of the gods chooses Enkidu, he falls ill, and after twelve days of increased suffering, finally dies. At first Gilgamesh refuses to believe that his friend has died. "What manner of sleep is this?" he asks poignantly. When he touches Enkidu's heart and finds that it does not beat, the terrible reality strikes home. "Then he veiled his friend like a bride. Storming over him like a lion," he recalls Enkidu's heroic prowess and sets up a statue to commemorate his lost companion. With the reality of Enkidu's death established in his consciousness, Gilgamesh sets off on the long and lonely journey to Utnapishtim, the Babylonian equivalent of Noah, hoping to learn from him the secret of immortality. Instead, he hears of the story of the great flood and Utnapishtim's role in it. Failing the test that Utnapishtim set for him to win immortality (he was unable to stay awake for seven nights), Gilgamesh comes to the dark realization that immortality is beyond human hope, and returns home to Uruk, a deeply saddened but wiser man.

Social Crisis

In setting forth the events that lead Gilgamesh to an awareness of his own mortality, the *Gilgamesh Epic* is careful to locate the hero in a social community. The story begins with Gilgamesh in the city of Uruk, and ends with his return to that same city. His departure from the city leads to wanderings, adventure, and ultimately, when he has gained the all-important lesson of human mortality, return to his original social setting. The tale clearly contains the pattern of separation, liminality, and reintegration, providing the framework for the hero's growth in experience and wisdom.

At the outset of the story, there are clear indications of social crisis:

> *He runs wild with the young lords of Uruk through the*
> *holy places.*
> *Gilgamesh does not allow the son to go with his father;*
> *day and night he oppresses the weak –*
> *Gilgamesh, who is shepherd of Uruk of the Sheepfold.*
> *Is this our shepherd, strong, shining, full of thought?*
> *Gilgamesh does not allow the young woman to go to her*
> *mother,*
> *the girl to the warrior, the bride to the young groom.*
> (Tablet I. column ii.11–17)[3]

The text suggests the nature of Gilgamesh's oppressive behavior: he seems to be the leader of a group of wild young nobles who, in some way or another, have been violating the gods' sacred precincts. He oppressed the weak with unremitting labor (by the imposition of corvée duty, as some have suggested). The ironic question "Is this our shepherd, strong, shining, full of thought?," indicates that he failed to provide the traditional leadership expected of the "shepherd" of the people. Finally, Gilgamesh violated sexual norms, not only with unmarried young women (still at home with their mothers), but also with the brides of the young nobles. It seems likely that he was exercising the *jus primae noctis* with the wives of his subjects. This practice was well known in the Middle Ages, and the testimony of Herodotus (4. 168) indicates that it was not unknown in antiquity as well.[4] This interpretation of Gilgamesh's behavior gains support when Enkidu first meets him and finds him on his way to a nuptial chamber:

> *Enkidu, at the gate of the bride house, planted his feet.*
> *He prevents Gilgamesh from entering.*

> *They seized one another in the bride-house gate.*
> (Tablet II. column ii. 46–48)

Enkidu's role here is that of "spoiler" as Gilgamesh is apparently exercising his kingly "right" to sleep with a bride. The meeting, then, of Enkidu and Gilgamesh is set in the context of the social crisis occasioned by the king's sexual misbehavior.[5]

At the core of the social crisis is the king's ambiguous status. Betwixt and between, he is both the upholder and the violator of social order. Because he is not constrained by the norms of society, he seems a liminal figure. From the functional perspective of myth and ritual, Gilgamesh's liminality sets the poem's main concern of life and death within the context of a social crisis. Although Gilgamesh is still having too much fun to be aware of his personal testing to come, his social ambiguity, along with its implications for the city, sets the stage for the poem's further development of these themes. To be specific, the social crisis at the poem's beginning leads to two important developments: first, it sets into motion the events that lead to the creation of Enkidu, his humanization, and his first encounter with Gilgamesh. Second, by suggesting Gilgamesh's liminal status, it also anticipates the changes to come in his understanding of himself and his place in the world.

Enkidu and the Liminal

When the subjects of Gilgamesh, chafing under his oppressive ways, seek redress from the gods, they send Enkidu. Tigay sees in this the common mythic pattern of "oppression, outcry, and divine response." Typically, an act of oppression results in complaint by the victims, in response to which the gods create someone to put an end to the oppression. For the poet of the *Gilgamesh Epic,* "it was a useful device for the introduction of Enkidu."[6] This pattern of oppression, outcry, and divine response also embraces another pattern, which I would term mythic liminality, and which is

related to the ritual patterns Eliade and van Gennep have investi-
gated. The prayers of the oppressed people of Uruk to Aruru are a
ritual response to social crisis, and the creation of Enkidu is a type
of hierophany. Appearing in the wilderness, the realm of the
profane, Enkidu enters the sacred center, that is, the city of Uruk,
bringing great changes to both Gilgamesh and his city. The
meeting of these two liminal figures leads to a number of liminal
confrontations with the chaotic.

Gilgamesh and the Liminal

Implicit in the hierophany-like coming of Enkidu is the question of civilization. Scholars have noted in the *Gilgamesh Epic* the
thematic contrast of nature and civilization. While Gilgamesh is a
man of the city, Enkidu is born on the steppe, the desert wastes,
and feeds on the grass with the animals and drinks with them at
their watering places. He is as wild and barbaric as Gilgamesh is
sophisticated and urbane.[7] The relationship between Gilgamesh
and Enkidu, especially as it develops in the early part of the epic, is
more than a simple friendship between two heroic males, but
rather has a much broader contextual significance. G. S. Kirk[8] has
examined the meaning of this relationship using the critical
categories of classical Greek scholarship, and interprets the
relation under the rubric of a *nature/culture* dichotomy. The
conflict of two individuals representing Nature and Culture sets
forth the themes of nature's subordination and domestication
through the humanizing effect of culture and civilization.

As has already been suggested, the contrast also has religious
and ritual dimensions: as king, Gilgamesh is *sacred*, while Enkidu,
standing outside of the city and its culture, is *profane*. Just as the
city, as the realm of order and as the extension of the temple, is
sacred, so too, the king, as the concrete representative of that
order, is also *sacred*; outside the city is the *profane*, the disor-

dered, the *chaotic*.   In tune with the world of nature, Enkidu roams the wilderness with the wild animals.

The coming of the liminal Enkidu to Uruk, the sacred center, is a type of hierophany, that is, a movement from the profane to the sacred, just as Gilgamesh's going in the reverse direction, when he goes in search of adventure and meets the monster Huwawa, is a movement from the sacred to the profane.   Gilgamesh, as emblematic of social order, also represents the initiated, while Enkidu is the uninitiated (or perhaps better, *the not yet initiated*) outsider. Thus, Enkidu is liminal. It is worth noting that these polarities are fluid, and change, as the two heroes become friends. At this point, however, the contrasts serve to point up the poem's larger mythic perspectives. Specifically, the meeting of Gilgamesh and Enkidu symbolizes the subordination of nature's wildness and chaos, which can be read as a thematic variant of our mythologem: the cosmic Gilgamesh meets and subdues the chaotic Enkidu. This, then, is the process that domesticates and humanizes the wildness of nature Enkidu represents.

There is, however, an important intermediate stage in the humanization of Enkidu, his seduction by the temple prostitute. When Gilgamesh learns how Enkidu has frustrated the hunters by filling in their pits and tearing out their traps to help the animals escape, he orders that a "love-priestess, a temple courtesan" be taken to the place where Enkidu waters the animals:

> *Have her take off her clothes, let her show him her*
> *strong beauty.*
> *When he sees her, he will come near her.*
> *His animals, who grew up in the wilderness, will turn*
> *from him.*
> (Tablet I. column iii.22–24)

The plan works; Enkidu, the *man-as-he-was-in-the-beginning* (to use Gardner's suggestive translation) is seduced by the prostitute's beauty, and learning "what a woman is," he spends six days and seven nights making love to her. However, there is a price to pay: when Enkidu returns to the animals of the wilderness, they flee, and he lacks the strength to pursue. Yet, as the poet observes, he has "knowledge and a wider mind." He has become human.

To understand the prostitute's role in the humanization of Enkidu, it is necessary to consider her social role. Temple prostitution often involves a rite of passage, by which the community incorporates a stranger into its social fabric. Coitus becomes the symbolic act of union and identification.[9] The sacred prostitute is the impetus for Enkidu's movement from liminality to incorporation. Enkidu's incorporation into the community of Uruk is also an entering into the larger community of human society as well.

There is also a religious dimension. Temple prostitutes were often identified with a goddess (Inanna, Ishtar, or Aphrodite), and as such were mediating figures.[10] It is significant that the prostitute identifies the city for Enkidu as "the holy place of Anu and Ishtar." She and the sexuality she represents mediate the profane status of Enkidu and the sacred status of the city.

This explains, at least partially, how sexuality, especially when personified by Aphrodite, Ishtar, or Inanna, is a civilizing power. In ancient and primitive cultures generally, sexuality has close connections with religion and magic; it involves strange, mysterious rituals of initiation, which lead to ecstatic experiences. From this perspective, Enkidu's encounter with the temple prostitute takes on characteristics of a spiritual encounter. She represents the primal mystery of procreation. We have, then, a mythic actualization of the *hieros gamos*, the ritual reenactment of a primordial theophany. Sexual ecstasy becomes another manifestation of the sacred hierophany, and is ritually reenacted by Enkidu (with little prompting needed, we may surmise, from the gods). As a result, Enkidu grows in spiritual perceptivity and wisdom.

This spiritual perceptivity is a type of knowledge, a sacred *gnosis* ("knowledge" is of course a well-established metaphor for sexual intercourse). The prostitute provides for his acquisition of knowledge, indeed crucial knowledge. As liminal initiands receive important tribal lore as part of their rituals of initiation, so also Enkidu, with the learning imparted by the knowing prostitute, moves beyond the limits of his *natural* existence and discovers his own innate potential for sacred knowledge. With this knowledge, his worldview expands far beyond its former limits, and he aspires to transcend the limits of his own being.

Because sexuality also involves the origins of life and the propagation of the race, it also involves the continuity of society and the development of culture. Hence, sexual consciousness and sexual relations are an integral part of socio-structural relationships. This explains the connection between the sexualization and socialization of Enkidu; simply put, the prostitute makes him a social being.[11] This social awareness plays an important role in his eventual meeting and struggle with Gilgamesh. (It explains Enkidu's indignation at Gilgamesh when, at their initial meeting, he discovers that Gilgamesh is on his way to a tryst.)

The important point is that both the spiritual and cultural dimensions of the prostitute's sexuality are at work in Enkidu's growth into humanity. His realization of the spiritual nature of his encounter with the prostitute comes at the point when the wild animals refuse to have anything more to do with him. She then makes the pronouncement: "You have become wise, like a god, Enkidu." This godlike wisdom is precisely the quality that defines being human. Not only does Enkidu become human, but because the prostitute represents divinity,[12] thus making possible his transcendent humanity, he also becomes heroic.[13] Being human and becoming heroic, however, have their cost. Enkidu soon learns the price of his socialization and humanization when he faces the reality of his own death.

Enkidu's experience with the sacred prostitute has profoundly changed him. The coming of the sacred prostitute to Enkidu in the wilderness represents the irruption of the sacred into the profane and initiates the process by which the liminal wild-man enters human society. All of this is from the perspective of Enkidu. In the eyes of Gilgamesh, however, Enkidu remains, despite his changed status and nature (of which Gilgamesh is necessarily ignorant), the liminal intruder coming from the realm of the chaotic and profane to threaten his position as king. The initial conflict between Enkidu and Gilgamesh, therefore, would naturally have all the characteristics of a heroic battle with the chaotic. Unfortunately, about forty-two lines have been lost, and the description of the actual battle is wanting.

That Gilgamesh is victorious is clear, and the two adversaries become fast friends. It is also clear that Gilgamesh too changes: in place of the self-centered tyrant imposing his will and his desires upon the residents of Uruk, we meet a Gilgamesh who sets out upon a heroic quest that begins the process of growth into heroic stature. Naturally implicit in this process is also *his* increasing humanization, as he becomes more aware of other dimensions of his humanity, especially in his relationship with Enkidu. He too will move from liminality to integration.

Huwawa

However, before that movement is complete, there is the conventional exploit of a battle with a monster or ogre. In assessing the significance of Gilgamesh's encounter with Huwawa, one can distinguish four levels of interpretation. On the historical, the journey to the mountain forest may reflect Sumerian expeditions to the surrounding hills to obtain the wood necessary for building projects in the city. Such expeditions would involve struggles with the inhabitants, whose claim of proprietary rights to the forest would lead to conflict between the city-dwellers and the hill-tribes.

There is in fact evidence of continuing warfare between Uruk and Aratta, a state in the Eastern hills.[14]   Second, one can read the episode simply as heroic adventure: two young men set out to win fame and glory by challenging the strange and powerful beings that lie beyond the horizon of the everyday world.[15]   The third level of interpretation may be termed the moral level: Huwawa is the personification of evil, and Gilgamesh is the knight who does battle with the evil dragon, to use the imagery of traditional folklore.   As is the case with many other stories of this type, the monster represents the primeval forces of chaos and annihilation,[16] and the heroic conflict with Huwawa becomes a symbolic battle with death.   This symbolism is clear from Enkidu's description of the monster:

> *To guard the [cedar forest]*
> *and to terrify mankind Enlil has appointed him,*
> *Humbaba: his shout is the storm-flood, his mouth, fire,*
> *his breath is death.*
> *He will hear the footsteps of a young man on the road*
> *[to the forest gate], anyone who goes up to the forest.*
> *To guard the cedar [forest] Enlil appointed him, and to*
> *make the people fear.*
> *Whoever goes up to the forest, weakness will come over*
> *him.*
> (Tablet II. column v.1–6)

In the Sumerian version of the epic, Huwawa is located in the "land of the living."[17]   His lair lies in the mountains—the Kur, a word which also means the underworld,[18] which not only stands apart from the ordered, inhabited world of human society, but also is the world of demons and devils, in short, the realm of death.[19]

Finally, there is the ritual level of interpretation.   The cedar forest is a liminal wilderness, where, like initiates being tested to prove their manhood, Gilgamesh and Enkidu must confront the monstrous Huwawa.   The episode also exhibits the bonding that

Turner calls *communitas*. The hero and his companion remove themselves from the realm of ordered society to enter a region of danger and chaos. The necessary interdependence and mutual egalitarianism of Gilgamesh and Enkidu establish human connectedness and community just at the point where it is most critical.

The expedition against Huwawa takes the heroes from the orderliness of the sacred center, the city of Uruk, to the wilderness, the profane and chaotic realm outside and beyond the order of the city, to do battle with the quintessence of the chaotic, personified in Huwawa, and raised to the level of deity.[20] Thus, this episode involves the pattern of ritual separation and liminal initiation, by which the heroic companions not only confront and defeat the powers of chaos, but also learns something about human mortality, the central theme of the poem.[21]

Gilgamesh's motivation in undertaking this quest is multivalent. On one level, he explicitly wishes to make a name for himself, that is, to establish his reputation and heroic identity. On another level Gilgamesh's quest involves him in bringing stability to the disordered, wresting order from chaos, thereby extending the limits of civilization. Like the Greek mythic hero Heracles, Gilgamesh becomes a cultural hero, whose adventures advance the cause of human community by eliminating what is inhuman and destructive.

Ishtar

However, before this pattern works itself out, another episode with its own mythic pattern intervenes. Ishtar offers Gilgamesh the opportunity to become her lover and husband:

> *To Gilgamesh's beauty great Ishtar lifted her eyes*
> *'Come, Gilgamesh, be my lover!*
> *Give me the taste of your body.*

> *Would that you were my husband, and I your wife!'*
> (Tablet VI. column i.6–9)

Nevertheless, Gilgamesh rudely spurns the goddess' invitation:

> *You're a cooking fire that goes out in the cold,*
> *a back door that keeps out neither wind nor storm,*
> *a palace that crushes the brave ones defending it,*
> *a well whose lid collapses,*
> *pitch that defiles the one carrying it,*
> *a waterskin that soaks the one who lifts it,*
> *limestone that crumbles in the stone wall,*
> *a battering ram that shatters in the land of the enemy,*
> *a shoe that bites the owner's foot!*
> *Which of your lovers have you loved forever?*
> (Tablet VI. column i.32–42)

In setting forth this litany of reasons for not submitting to the goddess, Gilgamesh uses examples of things that do exactly the opposite of their intended function. The effect of the multiplicity of examples he uses in his analogy is to universalize the destructive power of her deadly nature. In short, she turns things that are good and useful to bad ends. He then concludes his list of reasons for rejecting her offer by mentioning the well-known story of Tammuz, whose death was ritually mourned throughout Mesopotamia, and the story of her love of the shepherd, ultimately turned into a wolf and killed by his own dogs.²² Finally, he mentions her love of Ishullanu, her father's gardener, whom she turned into a frog:

> *to dwell in the middle of the garden,*
> *where he can move neither upward nor downward.*
> (Tablet VI. column ii.77–78)

These two examples indicate his fear that yielding to the love of Ishtar would lead to animalization and death. (The description of the frog suggests perhaps a ceramic garden decoration, beautiful to behold, but unmoving and dead all the same.)

First, it is noteworthy that this episode with Ishtar echoes Enkidu's encounter with the temple prostitute earlier in the epic. Yet Gilgamesh, unlike Enkidu, refuses, anticipating, it seems, the likelihood that, were he to accept Ishtar's offer, he would suffer a fate like that of Tammuz or the gardener, i.e., transformation into an animal. Second, there are clear undertones of the sacred marriage ritual (*hieros gamos*); indeed this part of the *Gilgamesh Epic* may have been modeled on such Mesopotamian rituals.[23] According to surviving texts, it seems that the king represented the fertility god Dumuzi/Tammuz and married a woman representing the fertility goddess Inanna/Ishtar in order to promote the fertility of the land.[24] In her attempt to seduce him, Ishtar promises Gilgamesh fertility for himself and his realm:

> *Mountains and lands will bring their yield to you.*
> *Your goats will drop triplets, your ewes twins.*
> (Tablet VI. column i.17–18)

If it is *sacred marriage* that Ishtar here offers, that is, a kind of incorporation ritual, we need to ask about the nature of the incorporation she is offering. Where earlier, through the sacred prostitute, Enkidu was offered entrance into humanity and civilization, Gilgamesh's insulting rejection of Ishtar suggests that his situation is very different from that of Enkidu. His critique of the goddess' previous encounters with mortal lovers makes clear both the difference and the danger: the *loss* of his humanity and death. The explanation then of Gilgamesh's tactless treatment of Ishtar lies in the pattern of what might be called "saying no to the goddess." Simply put, a goddess offers marriage to a mortal hero, whose refusal leads to dire consequences either for himself or for others connected to him. It represents the ultimate crisis in the ritualistic life of a traditional society, i.e. the failure of the sacred marriage, the concomitant failure of fertility, and the arrival of death for both the king and his realm. The crisis of ritual often comes just at the point when the hero has overcome all other barriers and dispatched all the monsters standing in his way. It is the final test of his heroic mettle.

Van Nortwick writes of Ishtar's offer and Gilgamesh's refusal in this way:

> Though Ishtar does not explicitly hold out the promise of immortality to Gilgamesh, she seems to raise the issue by offering something akin to the life of the gods. His response, a seamless extension of his heroic self-assertion, rejects by implication the possibility of immortality: she seems to extend a hand across the boundary between humans and gods, but this looks to him like an invitation to go in the other direction, from man to animal. Gilgamesh's current way of seeing precludes even considering the prospect of immortality, not because humility dictates he let go of that hope, but because his arrogance blinds him to the reality of death.[25]

It is, moreover, both a social and an individual crisis for the hero. Campbell describes it thus:

> This is the crisis at the nadir, the zenith, or at the uttermost edge of the earth at the central point of the cosmos, in the tabernacle of the temple, or within the darkness of the deepest chamber of the heart.[26]

Although it is not entirely clear what Campbell's imagery actually means, it well conveys, nevertheless, the emotional elements involved in the pattern. The rejection of divinity is always fraught with terror, and the goddess' reaction is predictable enough:

> *When Ishtar heard this*
> *Ishtar was furious and flew up to the heavens*
> *and went before Anu the father.*
> *Before Antum, her mother, she wept.*
> *'Father, Gilgamesh has insulted me.'*
> (Tablet VI. column ii.80–84)

This episode with Ishtar has echoes in the *Odyssey* both when the powerful Circe tries to seduce the hero Odysseus, who fears her power to turn men into animals, and when another goddess, Calypso, offers him immortality as her consort, if only he would stay with her and forget his homecoming. That refusal, incidentally, is thematically connected to Odysseus' various troubles on the sea, that is, the shipwreck of his raft by the anger of Poseidon. (Cf. the discussion below, chapter 4.)

In the case of Gilgamesh, the consequences are not fatal for himself but for Enkidu. A council of the gods determines that Enkidu must die. It will not be, however, a heroic death in battle, but a slow, lingering death by disease. When Enkidu dies, at first Gilgamesh refuses to accept its reality. Recounting all their glorious deeds, he concludes with a plaintive cry:

> *We who have conquered all things, scaled the moun-*
> *tains,*
> *Who seized the Bull,*
> *Brought affliction on Humbaba,*
> *What now is this sleep that has laid hold on thee?*
> (Tablet VIII column ii)[27]

When the truth of Enkidu's death finally sinks into Gilgamesh's consciousness, his reaction is a mixture of tender solicitude and animal rage:

> *He touched his heart, but it does not beat.*
> *Then he veiled his friend like a bride,*
> *Storming over him like a lion,*
> (Tablet VIII column ii)[28]

Enkidu's transition from the world of the living to the world of the dead is expressed in imagery of a wedding, the bride's ritual passage from one social position to another. Yet, as Kirk notes,[29] it is the wrong rite of passage. Funeral ritual is called for here, not rites of marriage. This ritual inappropriateness, together with the bold contrast of images, suggests that the author of the *Gilgamesh Epic* understood instinctively that, while the aim of funeral rituals is to ease the pain of the bereaved, Gilgamesh is beyond such comfort, when he irrationally chooses the wrong ritual.

Moreover, not only does Gilgamesh use the wrong ritual, he also undergoes his own passage from the human to the animal realm.

> *Like a lioness whose whelps are lost*
> *he paces back and forth.*
> *He tears and messes his rolls of hair.*
> *He tears off and throws down his fine clothes like*
> *things unclean.*
> (Tablet VIII. column ii.19–22)

The identification of Gilgamesh with a lioness and his tearing off his clothing suggest animalization, a loss of humanity, which makes clear the similarity between Enkidu, the once wild-man now dead, and Gilgamesh, whose grief removes him from the sphere of human relationships.[30]   Gilgamesh's expression of intense grief reminds one of Achilles' extreme reaction to the death of his companion, Patroclus. Like Achilles, Gilgamesh now perceives that he too will die, and the focus of this perception—his awareness that Enkidu's heart is not beating—is symbolically and dramatically analogous to Achilles' actions, when he stretches himself out full on the ground and, in a ritual act of self-inhumation, covers himself with dust (*Il.* 18.22–27). The death of Enkidu, then, is the event that forces Gilgamesh to confront his own mortality.[31]

In all of this, we recognize Enkidu's consistent role as an agent of liminality. Moving out of the realm of liminality into civilized society, he comes from the wilderness to the city and joins with Gilgamesh, which brings a new, unknown dimension to his life. He also returns to the liminal realm when he stirs in Gilgamesh the desire for adventure, and leads him from the city back to the wilderness to confront the chaotic Huwawa. His death leaves Gilgamesh profoundly alone, compelling him also to confront the liminality of death. Driven by his fear of dying, Gilgamesh journeys even further beyond the pale of human community, making his way to the underworld.

As with many mythic descents to the nether world, the description of Gilgamesh's actions is an external representation of an inner experience. All such mythic journeys to the land of the dead bring new insights, increased wisdom, and a more complete apprehension of truth. Utnapishtim, moreover, is more than merely a distant relative of Gilgamesh, as he too becomes an agent of liminality for Gilgamesh. He reinforces Gilgamesh's growing awareness of his own mortality, not merely as a rational fact, but a central part of his human existence. Gilgamesh now apprehends his mortality existentially, that is, as something integral to his very being.

Van Nortwick well limns this inner meaning of Gilgamesh's journey:

> So begins a version of the definitive heroic adventure, the trip to the underworld. To look death in the face and return to the living is the ultimate proof of a hero's extraordinary stature. On another level, the journey often represents a going into the dark places of oneself, to find certain truths hidden from us in our conscious life. Certainly, Gilgamesh's trek beyond the Twin Mountains and over the waters of death has this dimension, an acting out of the 'dying unto self'. He goes to the underworld... to discover how to escape being what he is, to escape death.[32]

Although Gilgamesh's long and lonely journey to Utnapishtim parallels the earlier journey to the wilderness to battle the chaotic and destructive monster Huwawa, it is also different. The geography of the second is eerie and otherworldly; it appears to be a spiritual landscape with nothing but allegorical meaning. The hero comes to the mountain passes at night, and kills two lions in the moonlight. This is a strange detail:[33] it is doubtful that the ancient Mesopotamians hunted at night; hunting lions is dangerous during the day, doubly so, one would think, at night. For the rest of the journey, until he reaches the Fountain of Youth, he wears the lion's pelt. Near Eastern archaeology has uncovered a large number of seals, portraying a figure in combat with lions, which is taken to be Gilgamesh; this seems a highly significant detail, yet its precise meaning is unknown.[34] On the basis of the Greek parallel provided by Heracles and his iconography, one may speculate that the lion skin has established an iconographic identity for Gilgamesh, based on and symbolized by this heroic exploit. The parallel to the Greek Heracles is instructive. As portrayed in Hesiod's *Theogony*, Heracles' heroic acts consist primarily of slaying primordial monsters such as Geryon (289– 94), the Lernaean Hydra (313–18), and the Nemean Lion (326– 32). The underlying conception of Heracles, consequently, is that of "a beneficent, regulatory force that fights against the disorderly and abnormal forces of nature which is in the process of being formed."[35]

Another connection to Enkidu suggests itself: earlier in the poem, Enkidu lived in the liminal wilderness with the animals; yet, this theriomorphic Gilgamesh kills animals in the wilderness. This implies that the liminality of Gilgamesh is of a different order than that of Enkidu. Here we are to understand Gilgamesh *struggling against* his liminal situation, rebelling as it were against his necessary rite of passage. This strange episode, then, suggests that Gilgamesh is doing battle not so much with the lions as with the night itself and the primeval, annihilating chaos it represents.[36] Gilgamesh has entered again a strange *liminal* world, where the demonic, nonsocial, and chaotic dwell. This time, however, he comes with a changed perspective. He now understands, in ways he did not before, the true nature of his adversary.

Thus, it is also possible to argue that the lions Gilgamesh slays represent death. Indeed, death is occasionally depicted as a wild animal. The chest of Kypselos, dated ca. 600 BCE and described in detail by Pausanias (5.17.5–19.10), portrays the figure of Death (Κήρ) as a sphinx-like woman with ferocious teeth, like those of a wild beast, and hooked nails on her fingers. It is important to note that one of the major aspects of Heracles' persona has to do with his struggles against death. When Achilles, for example, learns that Patroclus has fallen, in a scene that is one of the dramatic high points of the *Iliad*, he turns to a meditation on his own inescapable mortality and contemplates the mythic exemplum provided by Heracles:

> *For not even powerful Heracles escaped death* (κῆρα),
> *although he was dearest to Lord Zeus, son of Kronos,*
> *but fate overpowered him, and Hera's baneful wrath.*
> (*Il.* 18.117–19)

Heracles, moreover, was widely invoked by the ancient Greeks as the averter of the κῆρες, the spirits of death,[37] and the best example of this role occurs in Euripides' *Alcestis*, where he does actual battle with the god of death. Like Heracles, therefore, Gilgamesh, in this strange nocturnal fight with lions, struggles against the most chaotic and destructive element in human experience, death itself.[38] In sum, then, this episode establishes Gilgamesh as a prototype for Heracles. Slaying primordial monsters and battling the chaotic forces of nature, Gilgamesh also struggles with death, perhaps not so literally as Heracles in the *Alcestis*, yet with greater poignancy since, unlike Heracles, he is doomed to ultimate failure.

The Flood Theme

Gilgamesh's paradigmatic struggle with death is also connected to the story of the ancient hero Utnapishtim. Because Utnapishtim was the survivor of the great flood, and was rewarded with immortality, Gilgamesh's long and difficult journey to him gives the poet of the *Gilgamesh Epic* the opportunity to retell the story of the great universal flood. Like its Old Testament counterpart, this flood destroys all of humankind save a single man and woman who, known for their piety and goodness, alone are saved.[39] This is the epic's first explicit use of water to express the chaotic. At several points, the language of the narration suggests themes of chaos and battle:

> *Six days and seven nights*
> *the wind shrieked, the stormflood rolled through the*
> *land.*
> *On the seventh day of its coming the stormflood broke*
> *from the battle*
> *which had labored like a woman giving birth.*
> *The sea grew quiet, the storm was still; the Flood*
> *stopped.*
> (Tablet XI. column iii.127–131)

Although scholars seem agreed that much of the flood narrative in the *Gilgamesh Epic* was a later addition to the original Sumerian and Old Babylonian versions,[40] the addition is profoundly in tune with the underlying mythic patterns of the poem as a whole.[41] Utnapishtim is vital to the story because his role in the intellectual and spiritual growth of Gilgamesh makes him thematically central to the meaning of the epic. He is the one mortal who, because of his experience with the flood, and by virtue of his innate goodness, has been granted immortality and its attendant wisdom. He seems the best possible source of help to Gilgamesh in his need to confront death, and becomes a mythic pattern for Gilgamesh's own heroic development. This means that the struggles of Gilgamesh, as he traverses the wild and chaotic regions to make his way to Utnapishtim, form a mythic parallel to Utnapishtim's struggles with the wild and chaotic powers of the flood. The impulse, then, that brought Utnapishtim into the

Gilgamesh Epic took its start from the perception that both heroes struggled with the forces of chaos and destruction, and the earlier hero is used as a mythic exemplum for the latter.[42]

The importance of the flood theme, then, is that it establishes a kinship between Gilgamesh and Utnapishtim. When Gilgamesh first meets him, he is surprised by their similarity to one another, apparently expecting great differences between himself and this immortal and legendary hero:

> *I look at you, Utnapishtim.*
> *Your features are no different than mine. I'm like you.*
> *And you are not different, or I from you.*
> (Tablet XI. column i.2–4)

Anticipating, it seems, notable and visible differences between himself and this ancient immortal, he finds instead a visible similarity of features that belie his expectations. He notices, moreover, an element of laziness in his heroic temperament, when he remarks:

> *Your heart burns entirely for war-making,*
> *yet there you are, lying on your back.*
> *Tell me, how did you stand in the Assembly of the Gods,*
> *asking for life?*
> (Tablet XI. column i.5–7)

It is hard to avoid in these words Gilgamesh's incredulity. The putative heroic stature of Utnapishtim, that is, his zeal for warfare, is contradicted by his supine indolence: "There you are, lying on you back;" Gilgamesh seems to be saying to himself, "what kind of hero is this!" This incredulity continues with the seemingly sardonic "Tell me, how did you stand in the Assembly of the Gods?"

The explanation for Gilgamesh's incomprehension lies in the fact that Utnapishtim, like Gilgamesh, and unbeknownst to him, is also a liminal figure. (Similarly, when he first met Enkidu fresh

from the wilderness, he did not fully comprehend *his* nature.)
This liminality becomes clear when, in his answer to Gilgamesh,
he speaks of his separation from human community when the god
Ea (Sumerian Enki) enjoins him to deceive his townsmen with
subtle and ambiguous words:

> *You, you may say this to them:*
> *'Enlil hates me—me!*
> *I cannot live in your city*
> *or turn my face toward the land which is Enlil's.*
> *I will go down to the Abyss [Apsu], to live with Ea, my*
> *lord.*
> *He will make richness rain down on you—*
> *the choicest birds, the rarest fish.*
> *The land will have its fill of harvest riches.*
> *At dawn bread*
> *he will pour down on you—showers of wheat!'*
> (Tablet XI. column i.38–47)

We note the theme of social separation as Utnapishtim finds
himself an outcast from the city. He will also descend to the
nether world, the *Apsu*. (This is the realm of Enki, the god of the
subterranean waters.) Finally, like many another liminal individual, he becomes a figure of trickery and clever deception, as he
uses imagery of rain and flood to deceive his fellow townspeople
into believing that overflowing wealth and abundant prosperity
will rain down upon them.

Thus, Utnapishtim's liminality reinforces his kinship with Gilgamesh. This liminal connection reinforces the parallel between
Gilgamesh's struggle with death and Utnapishtim's struggle with
the chaotic sea. Thus, the flood narrative is conceptually central to
the *Gilgamesh Epic* as a mythic pattern of heroic conflict with the
chaotic. The issue of the heroic struggle with mortality is reflected
in the flood part of the *Gilgamesh Epic* in two related ways. First,
Gilgamesh's quest for the secret of immortality leads him to
Utnapishtim. Second, rituals of death, which recur frequently in

the narrative, bring focus to the nature of Gilgamesh's quest. In traditional societies, the process of dying is almost universally a rite of passage; it is a movement from the known to the unknown, from the ordered to the chaotic, from the sacred to the profane. Throughout almost the whole of the epic, the status of Gilgamesh is liminal. Early in the poem, he left the city to confront Huwawa; he returns at its end after the arduous voyage to Utnapishtim. Thus, to use van Gennep's three-fold categorization, the epic narrative spends little time on the stages of *separation* and *reincorporation*. Since he is, in much of the poem, liminal both in conception and in geography, his liminal status is essential to his heroism. Outside and beyond the normal and orderly, his heroic quest leads him to the chaotic and the destructive, first in the episode with Huwawa and, then, in the trek to Utnapishtim.

In this way, the whole of the Gilgamesh *Epic*—especially by virtue of the centrality of Gilgamesh's liminality and his quest for the answer to mortality—becomes a metaphor for the confrontation with death; in the very act of seeking immortality, the hero is dying. Gilgamesh laments:

> *In fear of death I roam the wilderness. The case of*
> *my friend lies heavy in me.*
> *On a remote path I roam the wilderness. The case of*
> *my friend Enkidu lies heavy in me.*
> *On a long journey I wander the steppe.*
> *How can I keep still? How can I be silent?*
> *The friend I loved has turned to clay. Enkidu, the*
> *friend I love, has turned to clay.*
> *Me, shall I not lie down like him,*
> *never again to move?*
> (Tablet X. column ii.7–14)

The double repetition of "wilderness" and "the case of my friend" gives rhetorical force to his liminal terror. Not only does Gilgamesh come to recognize that he too will die, "never again to move," the expression of terror at its prospect indicates that he is prepared to hear and understand Utnapishtim's similar terror during the flood. Although Utnapishtim does not explicitly speak of his terror, his tears of relief are poignant evidence:

> *Six days and seven nights*
> *the wind shrieked, the stormflood rolled through the*
> *land.*
> *On the seventh day of its coming the stormflood broke*
> *from the battle*
> *which had labored like a woman giving birth.*
> *The sea grew quiet, the storm was still; the Flood*
> *stopped.*
> *I looked out at the day. Stillness had settled in.*
> *All of humanity was turned to clay.*
> *The ground was like a great, flat roof.*
> *I opened the window and light fell on my face.*
> *I crouched, sitting, and wept.*
> *My tears flowed over my cheeks.*
> (Tablet XI. column iii.127–137)

Hence, we have come to the point in the story where an emotional *communitas* is established between two powerful, heroic, and liminal figures, who come to recognize the commonality of their struggle with chaos. Although Gilgamesh's quest ends in failure—Utnapishtim's immortality is unique and cannot in any case be conferred on another—yet he returns home at the poem's end with greater understanding; he has plumbed the puzzle of life and death and returns from his liminal encounters a much more humane, and indeed wiser human being.[43]

Return and Reintegration

Gilgamesh's return to Uruk at the poem's end marks the end of his period of grieving for Enkidu. Since the expression of grief usually has ritual dimensions, and in many cultures is a rite of passage, Gilgamesh's return is both a passage out of grief as well as a social reincorporation after his sojourn in liminal darkness.

Gilgamesh's attempt to overcome death was in fact a form of denial. His refusal to accept the certainty of his own death is part of a larger pattern—the refusal to accept the reality of the chaotic. By now accepting the inevitability of his own death, Gilgamesh also accepts the fact that the chaotic is a part of his own history. To be sure, when he returns to Uruk from the wilderness, he leaves the chaotic behind, but in another sense, it is still with him, and its continuing presence at the core of his being is the measure of how much he has changed, how much more mature he is than when first we met him at the poem's beginning.

Insofar as death is a metaphor for the chaotic, it represents the three stages of Gilgamesh's spiritual development. First he defies it in true heroic fashion when he confronts Huwawa, then he denies it both in his excessive grief for Enkidu and the journey to Utnapishtim. Finally, by accepting its inevitability, he recognizes that it is an inseparable part of life. In this, we have the beginnings of a new kind of heroism, one based on an awareness of mortality, not as something that separates one from other humans, but as the bond, the inner kinship with all who must die.[44]

This new heroism of human connectedness finds its symbolic expression in the city wall of Uruk. The poem begins with the observation that Gilgamesh built the "wall of Uruk of the Sheepfold / the walls of holy Eanna," and concludes with Gilgamesh urging Urshanabi, the boatman, to inspect the craftsmanship of those same city walls (Tablet XI. Column vi. 304–305).[45] Thompson put the importance of the walls thus:

> Gilgamesh returns to his city, and in an *aria da capo* the court singer brings his audience back to a meditation on the walls of the city; the great epic ends with an acceptance of limitation and celebration of that form of delimitation, the walls. The man who has slain the spirit of

the forest [Huwawa] has not slain the monster of death;
the walls of the city may rise up against the desert, but
for how long no man can say and no poet sing.[46]

The symbolic importance of city walls here at the end of the poem as well as at its beginning, together with the concomitant emphasis on Gilgamesh's role in their construction, serves as a frame for the story and underscores Gilgamesh's liminality as the focus of the epic. Most of the action takes place outside of Uruk's walls, beyond the *limina* of the city, as Gilgamesh experiences removal and separation from his cultural roots. There is also a connection between the city's walls and Gilgamesh's concern with his mortality. For the city walls are "the only work of the hero that promised, even guaranteed his immortality."[47] Thus Gilgamesh has now returned whence he started and his heroic sojourn has come full circle. The pattern of separation, liminality, and reintegration brings newfound insights into the nature of human life, and provides a key to understand the poem's broader meaning.

Conclusions

It seems almost a universal fact that traditional cultures hold to the belief that the dead continue to exist in another form or another place. Not only does this belief occur in mythic stories, it is also found in the rituals that reenact and accompany the most important transitions in life. Birth, puberty, marriage, geographic relocation, grief—all of these are ritually and mythically reinterpreted in terms of death and vice versa. As Eliade writes:

> ...this paradoxical process discloses a secret hope, and
> perhaps a nostalgia of attaining a level of meaning where
> life and death, body and spirit, reveal themselves as as-
> pects or dialectical stages of one ultimate reality.[48]

Insofar as Death is a tangible and real manifestation of the fundamental nature of the chaotic, Gilgamesh's confrontation with death, seen as a rite of passage, as movement from the known to the unknown, from the ordered to the chaotic, from the sacred to the profane, is an exploration, a probing of the boundaries of chaos. While it is true that in one sense his mission is a failure, in another, wider sense, it is an intellectual and spiritual success. He has grasped in new and profound ways the natural limits of his own being. With his new and broader understanding of Death, he has also acquired a new and deeper understanding of Life.[49]

Notes to Chapter II

[1] See S. N. Kramer, "Epic of Gilgamesh and Its Sumerian Sources," *Journal of the American Oriental Society* 54 (1944), 8.

[2] G. S. Kirk, *Myth, its Meaning and Functions in Ancient and Other Cultures* (Berkeley: University of California Press, 1970), 135.

[3] This citation and all that follow are taken from John Gardner and John Maier, *Gilgamesh*, translated from the Sîn-leqi-unninni version (New York: Alfred A. Knopf, 1984).

[4] See Jeffrey H. Tigay, *The Evolution of the Gilgamesh Epic* (Philadelphia: University of Pennsylvania Press, 1982), 187 for the relevant citations.

[5] It is also possible that Gilgamesh was confiscating wives, as Tigay notes (183), citing David's behavior with Bathsheba and Abraham and Isaac's concerns about the kings of Egypt and Gerar (Gen. 12.11–12; 20.11; 26.7).

[6] Tigay, 180. Tigay also finds the pattern in the Old Babylonian *Atrahasis Epic* where the Igigi-gods are oppressed day and night by the Anunnaki-gods; their complaints result in the creation of man, who replaced the enslaved gods in their labors. Similarly in the *Stele of the Vultures,* the complaint that the city of Umma was encroaching on the fields of Lagash leads the god Ningirsu to create the king Eannatum to deal with Umma. The earliest examples of this pattern occur in contexts dealing with the creation of man. It is also to be found in the O.T. Exod. 1–4; Judges 2.14–18; 3–9.

This pattern also occurs in Greek epic literature. At the beginning of the *Iliad* the priest of Apollo, Chryses, complains of his mistreatment by Agamemnon, and as a result, the god sends a plague against Agamemnon and the Achaeans. In the *Odyssey* Polyphemus, angered at being blinded by Odysseus, prays to Poseidon who sends a fearsome storm against the hero.

[7] Kramer, "Epic of Gilgamesh," (note 1 above), 9.

[8] G. S. Kirk, *Myth, its Meaning and Functions* (note 2 above), 132 ff.

[9] Cf. A. van Gennep, *Les Rites de Passage*, 48: "Le coït est nettement... un acte d'union et d'identification."

[10] The Akkadian terms *harimtu* and *shamhatu* both mean prostitute and were often used as epithets of the goddess Ishtar. Cf. Fontenrose, *The Myth of the Hunter and the Huntress* (Berkeley: University of California Press, 1981), 232, who argues that the "harlot is surely a form of Ishtar and parallels Aphrodite/Eos as well and Artemis in Greek myth."

[11] Susan Niditch, Chaos to Cosmos: Studies in Biblical Patterns of Creation (Chico, CA: Scholars Press, 1985), 42.

[12] As a sacred prostitute, she represents Ishtar; cf. Joseph Fontenrose, *The Myth of the Hunter* (note 10 above).

[13] That Enkidu has now become a hero is suggested by the boast at the end of the column: "I will call to him [Gilgamesh]; I'll shout with great force." Cf. Gardner, *Gilgamesh* (note 3 above), 80 note.

[14] N. K. Sandars, *The Epic of Gilgamesh* (New York: Penguin Books, 1972), 16. See also the Sumerian epic *Enmerkar and the Lord of Aratta* in Thorkild Jacobsen, *The Harps That Once—Sumerian Poetry in Translation* (New Haven: Yale University Press, 1987), 275–319.

[15] N. K. Sandars, *Gilgamesh, ibid.*, 32. This aspect of heroic adventure seems to be the dominant concern in the Babylonian version of this episode.

[16] Thomas Van Nortwick, *Somewhere I Have Never Traveled: The Second Self and The Hero's Journey in Ancient Epic* (New York: Oxford University Press, 1992), 21 observes: "The identification of Humbaba as evil, along with his position in the wild, indicates in fact that we have here an example of a very common motif in the Near Eastern hero story: the fight between the hero as agent of order and a monster representing chaos, disorder."

[17] This phrase is perhaps to be understood as a sardonic euphemism.

[18] Kramer, "Epic of Gilgamesh," (note 1 above), 13.

[19] The reader is referred to Mircea Eliade's description of "non-sacred space" in his *Images and Symbols* (*op. cit.*), 38, and the discussion of the same concept in D. H. Mills, "Sacred Space in Vergil's *Aeneid*," *Vergilius* 29 (1983), 36.

[20] A similar personification occurs in Vergil's *Aeneid* in the figure of Cacus, who is attacked and defeated by Hercules. This victory represents the imposition of order on chaos, hence the bringing of civilization.

[21] Frankfort, Wilson & Jacobson, *Before Philosophy* (Baltimore: 1946), 223.

[22] *Nomine mutato* we have here the pattern for the hapless Actaeon of Greek myth.

[23] Marriage is of course a rite of passage; for the ancient Sumerians the rituals of the sacred marriage were broadened beyond simply the king and his wife (to be) to include the whole nation; indeed the whole cosmos was involved when the sacred marriage occurred at the seasonal transition from one year to the next, and was explicitly thought to guarantee the annual fertility of both the people and their crops. Cf. Kramer & Wolkstein, *Inanna Queen of Heaven and Earth: Her Stories and Hymns from Sumer,* (New York: Harper & Row, 1983), 124–5.

[24] Cf. Tigay, *Evolution* (note 4 above), 175.

[25] Van Nortwick, *Somewhere I Have Never Traveled* (note 16 above), 24. I am not persuaded that arrogance has "blinded" Gilgamesh. At this point in the story, Enkidu is still alive, and Gilgamesh, therefore, has had no real experience of death.

[26] Joseph Campbell, *The Hero with a Thousand Faces*, (Princeton, NJ: Princeton University Press, 1949), 109.

[27] James B. Pritchard, *Ancient Near Eastern Texts Relating to the Old Testament*, 3rd Ed. (Princeton, NJ: Princeton University Press, 1969) 88.

[28] Pritchard, *ibid.*

[29] Kirk, *Myth, its Meaning and Functions* (note 2 above), 149.

[30] Although the tearing of one's hair and the ripping of clothing are traditional gestures of mourning in the ancient Near East, the collocation of this image with that of the lioness indicates the poet's wish to associate grief with dehumanization. See Gardner, *Gilgamesh* (note 3 above), 189 note.

[31] M. David sees the clear connection between Enkidu's death and Gilgamesh's confrontation with his own mortality: La fin d'Enkidu est avertissement, puisqu'elle atteste la puissance de la décision divine et la

menace du courroux divin sur Gilgamesh. Celui-ci semble supposer qu'
Ut-napishtim, consulté, lui donnera conseil ou moyen permettant de
tourner ou d'esquiver la règle du destin de mort. Le récit acquiert dès lors
une tension nouvelle: par cette voie précise, Gilgamesh obtiendra-t-il
tout ce qu'il désire? ("Le Récit du Déluge et L'épopée de Gilgames," in
Garelli, Gilgames et sa Légende [Paris: Librairie C. Klincksieck, 1960],
156.)

[32] Van Nortwick, *Somewhere I Have Never Traveled* (note 16 above), 28.

[33] The text is quite fragmentary at this point.

[34] Cf. Sandars, *Gilgamesh* (note 14 above), 36.

[35] Karl Galinsky, The Herakles Theme: the Adaptations of the Hero in
Literature from Homer to the Twentieth Century (Totowa, NJ: Rowman
and Littlefield, 1972), 68.

[36] Galinsky, Herakles, ibid.

[37] Galinsky, *Herakles, ibid.*, 14.

[38] For the Assyrian iconography of Gilgamesh as slayer of lions, the
reader is referred to G. Offner, "L'Épopée de Gilgamesh, a-t-elle été fixée
dans L'Art?" in Garelli (note 31 above), 175–181.

[39] In the Sumerian literature as in the Old Babylonian writings, the gods
send flood and deluge along with other catastrophes as a means of
punishing humankind. See Sandars, *Gilgamesh* (note 14 above), 14.

[40] J. H. Tigay, *Evolution* (note 4 above), 216 argues that the *Atrahasis
Epic* served as the source for Tablet XI (the flood narrative) of the latest
(Akkadian) version. Nevertheless, the Old Babylonian version "told how
Gilgamesh journeyed to Utnapishtim, the survivor of the flood" even
though "there is good reason to believe that the full story was not a part
of the epic before the late version," *ibid.*, 214.

[41] M. David, "Le Récit du Déluge" (note 31 above), 154 argues for
"l'existence d'un *rapport voulu* entre tabl. XI et tabl. I–X de la version
ninivite." (My italics)

[42] Homer does something similar in the *Iliad* when, in the episode of the
embassy to Achilles, he has Phoenix try to mollify the hero's anger by
narrating the story of Meleager and his destructive anger.

[43] B. Landsberger, "Einleitung in das Gilgames-Epos" (in Garelli note 31 above), 35 writes of this dimension of the poem's meaning: wenn Gilgamesh am Ende dieses ergebnislosen Kampfes von seiner Weltreise zurückkehrt, erscheint er als ein Gott der Weisheit, der den Babyloniern alles erklären kann und mit allen Dingen vertraut ist.

[44] Van Nortwick, *Somewhere I Have Never Traveled* (note 16 above), 32.

[45] Most scholars agree that Tablet XII is a much inferior later addition to the poem, and therefore understand the poem to end with Tablet XI.

[46] William Irwin Thompson, The Time Falling Bodies Take to Light: Mythology, Sexuality and the Origins of Culture (New York: St. Martin's Press, 1981), 205.

[47] Leo A. Oppenheim, *Ancient Mesopotamia: Portrait of a Dead Civilization* (Chicago: University of Chicago Press, 1977), 257.

[48] Mircea Eliade, "Mythologies of Death: An Introduction," *Religious Encounters with Death*, edited by Frank E. Reynolds and Earle H. Waugh (University Park, PA: Pennsylvania State University Press, 1977), 19.

[49] See Eliade's reference to and interpretation of Martin Heidegger's concept of "Freedom-unto-Death" (*Freiheit zum Tode*) in his "Mythologies of Death," 21–22. Cf. also B. Landsberger (note 43 above), 36: So erweist sich das Gilgamesh-Epos als Spiegel des Lebens eines einzigen grossen Mannes, als ein Sinnbild des menschlichen Lebens.

※

Chapter III
Achilles and the Scamander

In the twenty-first book of the *Iliad*, the Greek hero Achilles does battle with the Scamander, Troy's divine, tutelary river. The narrative tells how the personified river seeks to protect the Trojans, whom Achilles has been pursuing and slaughtering with violent abandon. Finally, the river rises in anger like a flood and attempts to destroy the hero:

> Ἦ, καὶ ἐπῶρτ᾽ Ἀχιλῆϊ κυκώμενος, ὑψόσε θύων,
> μορμύρων ἀφρῷ τε καὶ αἵματι καὶ νεκύεσσι.
> πορφύρεον δ᾽ ἄρα κῦμα διιπετέος ποταμοῖο
> ἵστατ᾽ ἀειρόμενον, κατὰ δ᾽ ᾕρεε Πηλεΐωνα.
> (21.324–27)

> *[The river] spoke and rose turbulent against Achilles, boiling upward, / muttering in foam and blood and dead bodies. / Then the purple billows of the rain-swollen river, / rising high, stopped and caught the son of Peleus.*[*]

This almost surrealistic conflict between mortal and chaotic deity is a variation of the common folklore motif of a hero's struggle with a river god. In the *Iliad,* it encapsulates the uniquely supra-human qualities of the hero, and the image of the river's anger, rising ever upward to a climax, reveals the chaotic forces at work both within Achilles himself and in the world without. (In the Homeric dialect, the participle κυκώμενος is used to describe both human emotion and the turbulence of waves, seas, and rivers.) As the anger of the river mirrors the anger in Achilles' soul, the struggle of mortal hero and divine river expands into a multivalent symbol of heroic conflict with the chaotic. Before considering further the implications of this scene, it will be useful

---

[*] Translations from the original Greek are the author's.

to consider the events that have led up to it, and the ways in which the poem gives expression to the idea of the chaotic.

As in the story of Gilgamesh and Enkidu, the death of his companion Patroclus compels Achilles to confront death. Also similar to the *Gilgamesh Epic* is Achilles' confrontation with death while in a state of heroic liminality, the result of his withdrawal from the war effort, and his growing alienation from his peers. Like the *Gilgamesh Epic*, the *Iliad* opens with social crisis, as Achilles comes into bitter conflict with Agamemnon. It is unlikely that these parallels are the result of conscious reminiscence, or direct literary influence; rather, they simply indicate, in the words of Van Nortwick, "how deeply embedded the story pattern is in the mythical substratum of the Mediterranean and the Near East."[1]

When the poem opens, the great war against the Trojans is in its tenth year and there is growing sentiment on both sides that the stalemate cannot continue. In his invocation to the Muse, the poet takes as his theme, not the war itself, but the story of Achilles' devastating anger and its consequences.

> Μῆνιν, ἄειδε, θεά, Πηληϊάδεω Ἀχιλῆος
> οὐλομένην, ἣ μυρί᾽ Ἀχαιοῖς ἄλγε᾽ ἔθηκε,
> πολλὰς δ᾽ ἰφθίμους ψυχὰς Ἄϊδι προΐαψεν
> ἡρώων,
> ...
> ἐξ οὗ δὴ τὰ πρῶτα διαστήτην ἐρίσαντε
> Ἀτρεΐδης τε ἄναξ ἀνδρῶν καὶ δῖος Ἀχιλλεύς. (1.1–7)
>
> *Sing, goddess, the wrath of Peleus' son, Achilles, / dev-
> astating, which inflicted pains thousandfold on the
> Achaeans, / and sent many strong souls of heroes to
> Hades ... since the time those two first stood in divisive
> conflict, / Atreus' son, prince of men, and godlike Achil-
> les.*

The initial cause of Achilles' anger is his conflict with Agamemnon, the commander in chief of the Achaean forces. Agamemnon has angered the god Apollo by keeping as the spoils of war the daughter of the god's priest. When the god visits a plague on the Greek camp, Agamemnon is compelled to relent, but claims compensation for his lost prize of honor; the Achaeans must give him another, and he takes Briseis, Achilles' prize of honor. In protest of Agamemnon's highhanded confiscation of the girl, Achilles withdraws from the fighting, and finds himself, consequently, increasingly isolated and alone. It is worth noting that the verb διαστήτην (*to stand apart*), which the poet uses to describe the quarrel, foreshadows the important idea of Achilles' separation and isolation.

The Moral Dimension

The consequences of Achilles' anger have recently been analyzed by Jonathan Shay, a psychiatrist working with Vietnam veterans suffering from Post Traumatic Stress Disorder (PTSD). In his book, *Achilles in Vietnam*, Shay argues for a number of parallels between the experiences of Achilles and those of American GIs who saw service in Vietnam. *Achilles in Vietnam* argues that PTSD originates in the sense of moral violation felt by soldiers, who experience not only war's brutality, but also a profound violation of their innate sense of moral order. The violation of this ethical sensibility leads to a loss of faith in the normative and common social values that are part of a culture's definition of right and wrong. Here Shay uses the Greek term *themis*, "what's right." The result of this violation is violent rage and social withdrawal on the part of those soldiers who see their moral world betrayed. Shay argues that Achilles' angry response to Agamemnon's highhanded treatment is paradigmatic of the experiences of many Vietnam veterans.

> ... but what has not changed in three millennia are violent rage and social withdrawal when deep assumptions of "what's right" are violated. The vulnerability of the soldier's moral world has increased in three thousand

years because of the vast number and physical distance
of people in a position to betray "what's right" in ways
that threaten the survival of soldiers in battle.[2]

Also at issue for Achilles is personal honor. Tied to material
possessions, honor is also, and more importantly, a matter of one's
standing among comrades and peers. To confiscate Achilles' prize
of honor—regardless of whether it be a woman or some other
valued possession—is to insult him deeply by lowering his standing in the society of his comrades. Achilles understands fully, even
if Agamemnon does not, the moral implications of losing Briseis:
he is wrongly being singled out as less deserving of honor. The
importance of this is twofold: Agamemnon's act and Achilles'
response have caused a serious crisis with both moral and social
implications; secondly, the process of Achilles' isolation has
begun, even before his withdrawal from the fighting and his threat
to return home.

Shay understands the important relationship between the social structures and the moral nature of military organization:

> Any army, ancient or modern, is a social construction de-
> fined by shared expectations and values. Some of these
> are embodied in formal regulations, defined authority,
> written orders, ranks, incentives, punishments, and for-
> mal task and occupational definitions. Others circulate
> as traditions, archetypal stories of things to be emulated
> or shunned, and accepted truth about what is praise-
> worthy and what is culpable. All together, these form a
> moral world that most of the participants most of the
> time regard as legitimate, "natural," and personally bind-
> ing. The moral power of an army is so great that it can
> motivate men to get up out of a trench and step into en-
> emy machine-gun fire.[3]

Achilles' sense of personal dishonor as a moral issue, then, is
closely connected to his expectations vis-à-vis the morality of the
whole military enterprise. Since Agamemnon has compromised
the integrity of the whole endeavor, Achilles believes that his own

integrity demands that he disassociate himself from it. While it may be argued that Achilles' response is not predicated on such moral reasoning, but is simply an emotional and unthinking reaction to a deep and hurtful insult, the poet, nevertheless, takes considerable pains to explore the moral issues involved, when, for example, the Achaean leaders send a deputation to Achilles in a vain attempt to persuade him to return to the fighting. The words of the emissaries and Achilles' response make clear the moral issues at stake: adequate compensation for the insult to Achilles' honor and—in Achilles' mind at least—the moral standing and motivation of Agamemnon himself.

In short, because of his quarrel with the commander in chief and his refusal to continue in the war effort, Achilles may have been able to claim the moral high ground; but he also loses status as he finds himself increasingly isolated and alone. This isolation, moreover, has implications for his mental well-being. The military context compounds the sense of abandonment and isolation, which, as Shay has argued, has deleterious effect upon a soldier's grasp of reality:

> Danger of death and mutilation is the pervading medium of combat. It is a viscous liquid in which every thing looks strangely refracted and moves about in odd ways, a powerful corrosive that *breaks down many fixed contours of perception and utterly dissolves others.* (my italics)[4]

Surrounded by the deadly chaos of war, and cut off from the support of comrades, soldiers like Achilles are profoundly vulnerable to psychological breakdown. The one thing at this point that offers Achilles some protection is the fact that he has withdrawn from the fighting and its dangers. With the death of Patroclus, however, that too will change.

Social Crisis and Heroic Liminality

It is important to keep in mind that, given the social and psychological setting of the *Iliad*, Achilles' refusal to fight represents a threat to the cultural and social stability of the Achaean camp. This threat is all the more serious because his is a society at war, and such social dislocations have far-reaching and disastrous consequences. To be sure, while the rank and file try to continue as though nothing has changed, nevertheless, Homer makes it clear through repeated allusions to Achilles' absence that there is considerable social tension, exacerbated in turn by the increasingly desperate military situation.

Achilles' awareness of the military consequences of his withdrawal increases his sense of psychological isolation, which reaches its high point with the death of Patroclus, his closest friend, and last remaining link to his erstwhile comrades. Achilles' reaction to the news of his friend's death is described in language that suggests death and burial:

> ἀμφοτέρῃσι δὲ χερσὶν ἑλὼν κόνιν αἰθαλόεσσαν
> χεύατο κὰκ κεφαλῆς, χαρίεν δ᾽ ᾔσχυνε πρόσωπον·
> νεκταρέῳ δὲ χιτῶνι μέλαιν᾽ ἀμφίζανε τέφρη.
> αὐτὸς δ᾽ ἐν κονίῃσι μέγας μεγαλωστὶ τανυσθεὶς
> κεῖτο, φίλῃσι δὲ χερσὶ κόμην ᾔσχυνε δαΐζων.
> (18.23–27)

> *[Achilles] seized in both his hands the grimy dust, / and pouring it on his head, defiled his lovely countenance; / black ashes settled on his nectar-sweet tunic. / He himself, in all his might, lay stretched out in the dust, with his hands tearing and defiling his hair.*

We have here the language of ritual: covering himself with dirt, Achilles enacts a symbolic burial. The precise sense of the Greek word τέφρη is *ashes*, suggesting also the ritual of cremation. Similarly, the tearing of hair is the traditional sign of funereal mourning.

These and other echoes of ritual activity have led several scholars to see patterns of ritual passage at work in Homeric poetry: Albert Lord[5] argues for a pattern of *withdrawal, devastation,* and *return.* On the basis of the same pattern, Michael Nagler[6] observes that in the *Odyssey* the hero's withdrawal and absence leads to the disjointing of the "entire social structure of Ithaca." Likewise, in the *Iliad* the withdrawal of Achilles from the fighting in the first book not only causes devastation, it also causes some "societal anarchy" especially at 13.109 and 14.49–51. Nagler also sees a threefold interlocking repetition of the withdrawal, devastation, and return pattern. Let it suffice to note that the Lord/Nagler pattern corresponds fairly closely to van Gennep's schema, when one interprets the middle stage of devastation as a particularized manifestation of the liminal hero's license to transgress the taboos of the society from which he is separated. (Cf. discussion pp. 77f. *infra.*)

Similarly, Mary Louise Lord in a study of the Homeric Hymn to Demeter[7], has identified six principal elements occurring and recurring; (1) withdrawal of the hero or heroine; (2) disguise during the absence or upon the return of the hero; (3) the theme of hospitality to the wandering hero; (4) the recognition of the hero, or at least a fuller revelation of his identity; (5) disaster during or occasioned by the absence; (6) the reconciliation of the hero and his return.

Here too it is possible to see an elaboration of van Gennep's simpler and more basic pattern. The first element corresponds to van Gennep's rite of separation; the second suggests the hero's liminality as he stands outside the bounds of customary social relations, and enjoys license to violate at will usual canons of behavior; the third also is part of the liminal stage in that the hero is recognized as extra-social by virtue of the hospitality extended him. Hospitality may also be part of the reincorporation stage. Similarly, the fourth and sixth items also point to reintegration;

lastly, the fifth item, like the theme of devastation in the Lord/Nagler schema is part of the liminal phase.

In considering van Gennep's formulation and its relevance to the *Iliad*, one must keep in mind the central conception that underlies his articulation of rites of passage, to wit, changes from one social status to another are always accompanied by ceremonial patterns; such social changes are conceptualized as movement or passage from one social position or rank to another, or from "one cosmic or social world to another."[8] Such changes, moreover, are not limited solely to ritual or religion, but are part of an inclusive pattern, embracing a wide variety of changes in the life of an individual and of a society.

In discussing the experience of change and its presence in all rites of passage, van Gennep writes:

> For groups, as well as for individuals, life itself means to separate and to be reunited, to change form and condition, to die and to be reborn. It is to act and to cease, to wait and rest, and then to begin acting again, but in a different way. And there are always new thresholds to cross: the thresholds of summer and winter, of a season or a year, of a month or a night; the thresholds of birth, adolescence, maturity and old age: the threshold of death and that of the afterlife for those who believe in it.[9]

In considering Achilles' isolation from his comrades, especially in the light of its similarity to ritual patterns, one must recognize that initially Achilles enjoys something of a leadership role; he is, for example, the one who summons the assembly to deal with the crisis of the plague (1.54), and he appears as the spokesman for the Achaeans in general. In addition, when the seer Calchas is on the point of revealing the source of the plague, to wit, Apollo's anger with Agamemnon, he turns to Achilles for support and protection against the king's anticipated angry reaction. As *Iliad* 1 unfolds, however, Achilles certainly separates himself from Agamemnon, but also from his fellow warriors as well. "Go ahead," he says to the king, "give these orders to the others; but for my part, me thinks I'll obey you no longer" (1.295). At issue, of course, is Agamemnon's authority, and Achilles' view of it differs not only from that of Agamemnon himself, but also from that of his fellow soldiers. They obey, Achilles does not.

Redfield has noted:

> In the story of Achilles, the poet dramatizes a fundamen-
> tal contradiction: communities, in the interest of their
> own needs, produce figures who are unassimilable, men
> they cannot live with and who cannot live with them.[10]

Such heroes find themselves on the margins of society, alienated from all social structures, and beset by suspicions of arrogance and hubris. This is precisely Achilles' situation. His status has changed and he stands in a new relation to his society's structures and points of authority. Because he is now outside of his community, it ceases to have authority over him. This is also the situation of the novice or initiand in van Gennep's description of liminality. As the usual ties to society are modified, sometimes broken altogether, the initiate stands outside of society and is no longer subject to its authority.[11] Achilles therefore is in the position of one about to make a transition, perhaps akin to that from childhood to maturity, a change not without considerable social and psychological dislocation.

Achilles' liminality, moreover, goes beyond that of Gilgamesh in that it transcends even human boundaries. This is suggested when Patroclus addresses Achilles in the sixteenth book, and when he returns to Achilles with news of how badly the Achaeans are faring without him. He also makes the fateful suggestion that he don Achilles' armor and enter the fray, causing the Trojans to think that Achilles himself has returned. Patroclus chides Achilles for his indifference to their suffering:

...σὺ δ' ἀμήχανος ἔπλευ, Ἀχιλλεῦ.
μὴ ἐμέ γ' οὖν οὗτός γε λάβοι χόλος, ὃν σὺ
φυλάσσεις,
αἰναρέτη· τί σευ ἄλλος ὀνήσεται ὀψίγονός περ,
αἴ κε μὴ Ἀργείουσιν ἀεικέα λοιγὸν ἀμύνῃς;
νηλεές, οὐκ ἄρα σοί γε πατὴρ ἦν ἱππότα Πηλεύς,
οὐδὲ Θέτις μήτηρ· γλαυκὴ δέ σε τίκτε θάλασσα
πέτραι τ' ἠλίβατοι, ὅτι τοι νόος ἐστὶν ἀπηνής.
(16.29–35)

*But you, Achilles, are impossible. / May no such anger
take me, as this anger you nurture; / Damn that virtue
of yours! What other man, though lately born, will en-
joy your help, / if you do not ward off from the Argives,
this disgraceful destruction? / You have no pity: your
father was not the horseman Peleus, / nor Thetis your
mother; the gray sea bore you, / and the towering
rocks, that your mind is so unfeeling.*

The imagery of gray sea and towering rocks suggests Achilles'
out-sized, non-human dimensions. There is something absolute
and uncompromising in Achilles that makes this a compelling
comparison. The cold, distant, and unfeeling connotations of the
imagery suggest that Achilles' remote and unfeeling detachment
from his comrades and his absolutist perspectives have removed
him from all human community.

Achilles' absolutism is expressed by the single word
αἰναρέτης. A compound of ἀρετή (*courage, virtue, excellence*)
and αἰνός (*dreadful, awful*), it means something like, *you are a
man of dreadful virtue*. This strange combination, a moral
oxymoron, if you will, suggests that Achilles has pushed his moral
sense beyond reasonable limits into the region of moral ambiguity,
if not even clear wrong.[12]

It is also ironic that Patroclus, the very one whose death leads
to the final stages of his alienation and separation, is the one to
point this out. The result of Patroclus' denunciation is naturally to
push Achilles even deeper into his isolation. This breech will be

complete and total when Patroclus himself dies. At this point, however, it serves to foreshadow the battle with the Scamander, which, as shall be seen, speaks to Achilles' transcendent heroism.

Achilles' heroic nature, almost by definition, puts him beyond the limits of ordinary mortals. For such an individual, social constraints are a nuisance at best, at worst a threat to his autonomy. As a powerful son of a goddess, moreover, he has the potential for great good and great harm. (Not unlike Oedipus, he is *sacer*, both a blessing and a curse to his own.) His attention is focused inwardly on his own honor and of necessity, his heroic nature lacks humility. All of this suggests his peculiar liminality: his isolation and alienation from both his comrades and society in general is the result of his inability to accept the human limitations of other men. As with Gilgamesh, his liminality becomes the source of poignant tragedy when he must confront the ultimate limitation of his heroic being, death itself.

Achilles at the Scamander

This confrontation with death receives its most telling expression in the twenty-first book when Achilles does battle with the Scamander, Troy's divine, tutelary river. A careful reading of this book reveals three stages in the hero's struggle with the chaotic river. In the first, Achilles pursues fleeing Trojans to the ford of the river, killing many, and reddening the river's waters with blood (1–21). In the second, he slays Lycaon and Asteropaeus, and in response, the river rises in anger against him (34–283). In the third, the gods come to the forefront: Poseidon and Athena encourage Achilles to stand against the river. When, however, the Scamander appeals for aid to his brother tributary, the Simois, Achilles finds himself all but swept away. When the goddess Hera calls upon Hephaestus, we witness an elemental battle between two opposing forces of nature, as the fire of Hephaestus overwhelms the flood. Scamander is forced to yield, and war breaks out among the gods: when Ares attacks Athena, she drops him with a stone and then wounds Aphrodite. Poseidon challenges Apollo, and Hera attacks Artemis (283–496).

The overall impression of the poetic movement during these strange events is one of increasing violence and chaos, which involves much of the natural world and the gods who are connected with it, both mythically and symbolically. All the same, the primary focus is the conflict between the hero and the river:

> Ἦ, καὶ Ἀχιλλεὺς μὲν δουρικλυτὸς ἔνθορε μέσσῳ
> κρημνοῦ ἀπαΐξας· ὁ δ᾽ ἐπέσσυτο οἴδματι θύων,
> πάντα δ᾽ ὄρινε ῥέεθρα κυκώμενος, ὦσε δὲ νεκροὺς
> πολλούς, οἵ ῥα κατ᾽ αὐτὸν ἅλις ἔσαν, οὓς κτάν᾽
> Ἀχιλλεύς·
> τοὺς ἔκβαλλε θύραζε, μεμυκὼς ἠΰτε ταῦρος,
> χέρσον δέ· ζωοὺς δὲ σάω κατὰ καλὰ ῥέεθρα,
> κρύπτων ἐν δίνῃσι βαθείῃσιν μεγάλῃσι.
> δεινὸν δ᾽ ἀμφ᾽ Ἀχιλῆα κυκώμενον ἵστατο κῦμα,
> ὤθει δ᾽ ἐν σάκεϊ πίπτων ῥόος· οὐδὲ πόδεσσιν
> εἶχε στηρίξασθαι· ὁ δὲ πτελέην ἕλε χερσὶν
> εὐφυέα μεγάλην· ἡ δ᾽ ἐκ ῥιζέων ἐριποῦσα
> κρημνὸν ἅπαντα διῶσεν, ἐπέσχε δὲ καλὰ ῥέεθρα
> ὄζοισιν πυκινοῖσι, γεφύρωσεν δέ μιν αὐτὸν
> εἴσω πᾶσ᾽ ἐριποῦσ᾽· ὁ δ᾽ ἄρ᾽ ἐκ δίνης ἀνορούσας
> ἤιξεν πεδίοιο ποσὶ κραιπνοῖσι πέτεσθαι,
> δείσας· οὐδέ τ᾽ ἔληγε θεὸς μέγας, ὦρτο δ᾽ ἐπ᾽ αὐτῷ
> ἀκροκελαινιόων, ἵνα μιν παύσειε πόνοιο
> δῖον Ἀχιλῆα, Τρώεσσι δὲ λοιγὸν ἀλάλκοι.
> (21.233–50)

> *And spear-famed Achilles sprang from the bank into the middle / of the water, but the river with boiling swells set upon him, / raising all its streams in turbulence, and piled up the many corpses, / which were all about, of those whom Achilles had slain; / bellowing like a bull, he thrust them out / onto the land, but the living he saved beneath his comely streams / hiding them deep within his huge eddies. / And around Achilles*

towered a swelling billow, foaming terror, its current falling on his shield, thrust against it; / he could not keep his footing; with his hands he snatched at an elm, / well grown and huge; but, toppling roots and all, / it pulled down the whole bank. It stopped up the river's comely streams / with its thick tangle of roots. It dammed the river itself, / falling full length into it. But Achilles, rising from of the swirling waters, / sped in fear to reach the plain in the quickness of his feet. / But the great god did not give up, but rose against him, / his waters' surface glimmering darkly, to end the labor / of god-like Achilles and fend destruction from the Trojans.

Leaping into the river, Achilles finds himself engulfed in a battle with the river god in a realm of watery liminality. This surrealistic description of the river's power underscores its ambiguous divinity, that is, its power both to destroy and to save. The divine river both seeks to hide and preserve his Trojans, and at the same time to destroy their persecutor. This liminal ambiguity is visually suggested by the descriptive participle ἀκρο-κελαινιόων (lit.: *growing black on the surface*): as the river's bright surface, glimmering with its swirling waters, turns ominously dark and sinister, we begin to sense that Achilles has overreached himself, misjudging the danger posed by his watery adversary.

All the same, the conflict between mortal hero and divine river suggests the strangely transcendent, almost superhuman power of the hero to move beyond the usual limits of humanity. This heroic movement beyond the human often finds expression in the language of divinity. Gregory Nagy, noting that the formula δαίμονι ἶσος (*equal to divinity*), is used to describe Achilles at the beginning of the encounter (21.18), goes on to observe: "this epithet traditionally marks the climactic moment of god-hero antagonism in epic narrative."[13] Achilles' struggle with the river rises to a higher, metaphysical level of meaning, as he becomes an expression of the universal human aspiration to divinity. This aspect becomes clear, first by Achilles' boast of descent from Zeus as proof of his superiority to the river:

αὐτὰρ ἐγὼ γενεὴν μεγάλου Διὸς εὔχομαι εἶναι.

...

τῷ κρείσσων μὲν Ζεὺς ποταμῶν ἁλιμυρηέντων,
κρείσσων αὖτε Διὸς γενεὴ ποταμοῖο τέτυκται.
(21. 187, 190–91)

But I boast that I am descended from great Zeus ... As Zeus is stronger than the rivers that flow to the sea, / so too a descendant of Zeus is become stronger than a river.

A second dimension of Achilles' battle with the Scamander, and which is of particular interest to this study, concerns the parallels with flood narratives in other Near Eastern literatures. As Michael Nagler writes:

> The river fight is best appreciated not only as a combat myth, which it is, but also as a flood story of the exact type that Sumerian and Babylonian documents have made dramatically familiar to scholars of Near Eastern civilization over the last two decades or more.[14]

Noting the general resemblance between the Scamander episode and the Atrahasis deluge as well as the specific details of language (bellowing like a bull), he also suggests that the Scamander, a river *daemon* remythologized into a deity of death, is "the anciently defeated chaos demon who lies at the source of all terrestrial waters."[15] The Scamander river, therefore, provides a functional parallel to Huwawa in the *Gilgamesh Epic*. Just as Gilgamesh and Enkidu confronted the chaotic monster in a liminal wilderness, so too Achilles meets his chaotic adversary in the midst of his swirling waters.

In the final stage of the river battle, moreover, Homer goes beyond the mythic pattern itself, and extends it to include a battle

between the elements. At the urging of Hera, Hephaestus, the god
of fire, enters the fray and confronts the river with his fiery power:

> ...῞Ηφαιστος δὲ τιτύσκετο θεσπιδαὲς πῦρ.
> πρῶτα μὲν ἐν πεδίῳ πῦρ δαίετο, καῖε δὲ νεκροὺς
> πολλούς, οἵ ῥα κατ' αὐτὸν ἅλις ἔσαν, οὓς κτάν'
> Ἀχιλλεύς·
> πᾶν δ' ἐξηράνθη πεδίον, σχέτο δ' ἀγλαὸν ὕδωρ.
> ...
> ...ὁ δ' ἐς ποταμὸν τρέψε φλόγα παμφανόωσαν.
> καίοντο πτελέαι τε καὶ ἰτέαι ἠδὲ μυρῖκαι,
> καίετο δὲ λωτός τε ἰδὲ θρύον ἠδὲ κύπειρον,
> τὰ περὶ καλὰ ῥέεθρα ἅλις ποταμοῖο πεφύκει·
> τείροντ' ἐγχέλυές τε καὶ ἰχθύες οἳ κατὰ δίνας,
> οἳ κατὰ καλὰ ῥέεθρα κυβίστων ἔνθα καὶ ἔνθα
> πνοιῇ τειρόμενοι πολυμήτιος Ἡφαίστοιο.
> (21.342–45, 349–55)

> *...and Hephaestus readied a god-kindled fire. / First he
> ignited a fire in the plain and burned the many /
> corpses which were all about, of those whom Achilles
> had slain; / all the plain was parched and the shining
> waters were stopped.*
> ...
> *Then he turned his brightly burning flame into the
> river. / The elms burned, and the willows, and the
> tamarisks, / the clover burned, and the rushes, and the
> sedges, all those plants that grew abundantly along the
> river's beautiful streams. / They suffered, the eels and
> the fish in the eddies / that plunged here and there be-
> neath the beautiful streams, / wearied by the blast of
> much-contriving Hephaestus.*

As Whitman has argued, the poem's recurring images of light
and fire point to the innate fire of Achilles himself and symbolize
his quest for the absolute.[16] Thus, the surrealistic conflict between
the river god and the fire of Hephaestus is not simply a mythic
theomachy, a fight between divine and personified forces of
nature; it also represents a struggle within Achilles himself. As

elsewhere, here too Homer projects inner psychological experience onto external natural phenomena, choosing what were for ancient man perhaps the two most terrifying of natural events, a river in flood and a raging conflagration.

Every encounter with the chaotic necessarily involves a profound fear of destruction and oblivion. Achilles sees the river rise against him and speaks of his terror in the face of a chaotic force with the power to annihilate him:

νῦν δέ με λευγαλέῳ θανάτῳ εἵμαρτο ἁλῶναι
ἐρχθέντ' ἐν μεγάλῳ ποταμῷ, ὡς παῖδα συφορβόν,
ὅν ῥά τ' ἔναυλος ἀποέρσῃ χειμῶνι περῶντα.
(21.281–83)

But now I am fated to be caught in a dismal death, / trapped in a big river, like a boy, a swineherd, / who is swept away by a torrent as he tries to cross during a winter storm.

His fears are well justified by the river's plan to bury him in perpetual oblivion; Scamander says:

... κὰδ δέ μιν αὐτὸν
εἰλύσω ψαμάθοισιν ἅλις χέραδος περιχεύας
μυρίον, οὐδέ οἱ ὀστέ' ἐπιστήσονται Ἀχαιοὶ
ἀλλέξαι· τόσσην οἱ ἄσιν καθύπερθε καλύψω.
(21.318–321)

And I will enfold him / deep in the sand, pouring gravel / uncounted, nor will the Achaeans know where to gather his bones; / with such a mass of mud down on top of him will I conceal his remains.

Achilles' terror in the face of the river's onslaught is part of the inner conflict Whitman calls the *heroic paradox*, the constraints of human mortality in antithesis to the hero's aspirations of divinity.[17] Achilles had earlier come face to face with mortality through the death of his dear friend, Patroclus (just as Gilgamesh had with the death of Enkidu), but Achilles' "urge toward divinity" has now, by reason of Patroclus' death, become much more than merely an aspiration: his impulse to divinity is tested by the chaotic force of the river, which again and again threatens to destroy him.

Homer portrays, then, the conflict between two terrible and irreconcilable absolutes in Achilles' temperament, as is suggested by the chaotic elements of the description. One absolute, the all-consuming and destructive fire, is the heroic will to be first, and to crush all that stands in the way of heroic self-actualization. The other is represented by water, which, like fire is ambivalent in its symbolism. On the one hand, its gentle and nurturing role (Scamander expresses his loving concern for the Trojans) points to the gentle bond of devotion between Achilles and Patroclus; on the other, it is the passionate, almost self-denying and self-destroying love of one comrade for another. As symbolized by the river this absolute becomes the destructive flood tide of anger when that love is negated by loss. The conflict of two absolutes is thus a conflict between self-love and the heroic bonding of two comrades in arms. Because the battle of elements expresses an internal conflict between two irreconcilables, it does not end in resolution, but finds its fulfillment in self-destruction. Achilles' all-destructive rage, despite its permutations from the beginning of the poem to the present battle with the Scamander, is directed finally inwardly against himself.

When seen, therefore, from the perspective of the entire poem, Achilles' battle with the chaotic reveals his human limitations both to us, and eventually to Achilles himself, especially when the poem brings into focus his inability to realize simultaneously two mutually exclusive absolutes. Not only is his situation incapable of resolution, and therefore a manifestation of the chaotic, it also leads inexorably to his destruction. While it is true that Achilles' death lies outside the purview of the *Iliad,* Homer has, all the same, so contrived his tale that we are well aware of the hero's eventual fate. Achilles' battle with the chaotic, when described in the language of conflict between fire and water, reveals the insight that the chaotic is in fact the inner reality of the heroic nature. It is the tension of this inner chaos that renders the hero, in Whitman's suggestive phrase, "too large for life," thus sealing his inevitable doom.

Inner Chaos and the Moral Center

This inner chaos of Achilles when he enters the river to battle Scamander has points of contact with what Johanthan Shay calls the *berserk state* in his book on the psychological experiences of soldiers who fought in Viet Nam. Shay sets forth the thesis that the betrayal of *themis*, "what's right," grief, guilt at the death of the special comrade, and the sense of being already dead, all combine to produce a psychological condition in which a soldier experiences feelings of supernatural power and invulnerability. Losing any sense of decent or moral conduct, he comes to believe that he is immune to death.[18] Shay lists the characteristics of the berserk state:

> Beastlike
> Godlike
> Socially disconnected
> Crazy, mad, insane
> Enraged
> Cruel, without restraint or discrimination
> Insatiable
> Devoid of fear
> Inattentive to own safety
> Distractible
> Indiscriminate
> Reckless, feeling invulnerable
> Exalted, intoxicated, frenzied
> Cold, indifference
> Insensible to pain
> Suspicious of friends[19]

As Shay makes clear, all of these characteristics apply to Achilles at various points in the *Iliad*; they all come together, moreover, in a profoundly moving metaphoric and symbolic synthesis in the episode of the Scamander. The contradictory impulses that defy logic and reason, the self-destructive behaviors that belie the confidence of invulnerability in one who is terror-stricken by the river's attack, seem expressible only through the imagery of an enraged divinity run amok.

Although Shay has fully described the external manifestations of the berserk state, he confesses all the same his ignorance about its physiological dimensions. Similarly, it is not hard to imagine that ancient warriors and poets, in recounting their ordeals, found it equally difficult to understand and describe the phenomenon of the berserk state. The poet of the *Iliad*, then, as poets have always done, turned to figurative and metaphorical language to give expression to the terrors of war. But he also goes farther in setting forth a surrealistic picture that combines a personified water deity and the abstract principle of fire itself entering into the conflict; this picture is the poet's way of portraying Achilles' extreme mental state.

There is one detail in Shay's account of PTSD which suggests that Achilles' encounter with the river is really about the relationship between soldiers' experiences and their memories of them. He writes about the traumatic flashbacks that many veterans of combat in Vietnam experience:

> Traumatic memory is not narrative. Rather, it is experience that reoccurs, either as full sensory replay of traumatic events in dreams or flash backs, with all things seen, heard, smelled, and felt intact, or as disconnected fragments. These fragments may be inexplicable rage, terror, uncontrollable crying, or disconnected body states and sensations, such as the sensation of suffocating in a Viet Cong tunnel or *being tumbled over and over by a rushing river*—but with no memory of either tunnel or river (my italics).[20]

The detail of being tumbled over and over in a rushing river is strikingly reminiscent of Achilles' struggle in the Scamander river. It follows, then, that this surrealistic encounter with the river is also a remembered experience. As the poet sings his song, he is aided by the Muse of memory, who calls up all the nightmares of returned soldiers, incorporating them into the story of Achilles' berserk rage. This helps explain Achilles' helplessness before the river's onslaught. The returned soldier does not merely remember the realities of war, he relives them and often is unable to stop or alter the reliving of the experience.

> We must bear in mind that when the traumatic moment reoccurs as flash back or nightmare, the emotions of terror, grief, and rage may be merged with each other. Such emotion is relived, not remembered. ...Once re-experiencing is under way, the survivor lacks authority to stop it or put it away. The helplessness associated with the original experience is replayed in the apparent helplessness to end or modify the reexperience once it has begun.[21]

The value of Shay's work lies in its attempt to relate Homer's description of Achilles' mental state to the psychological trauma suffered by his heroic warriors. The poet's efforts to understand and conceptualize Achilles' psyche, are also an attempt to fathom the effect of war upon its participants. Although Homer does not have the language and concepts of modern psychology, he does in fact, I would argue, employ the traditions of ritual passage and the mythic language, which, in its own uniquely metaphorical and stylized manner, addresses the very issue of war's effect upon its participants. In addition, the Scamander episode brings to bear a kind of surrealism that suggests not only the reality of the warrior's experience, but also, and more importantly, his later memories of it. Thus, the Scamander episode has something of a flashback quality to it. It is, as it were, the gripping story of a PTSD soldier as he recounts and reexperiences in the presence of his therapists his most recent nightmare. Did Homer know of such stories? It seems reasonable to suppose that the ancient bards of the epic oral tradition included in their repertoire the stories of returned soldiers, which no doubt could be and were embellished by the addition of details culled from their nightmares.

One can argue, then, that the poet fully understands the nature of his performance: he is not merely narrating events that happened long ago, but recreating them, causing his audience to experience, first hand as it were, the powerful emotions of those very soldiers, both as they initially experienced them, and then as they relive the uncontrollable terrors of their nightmares.

By so recasting the heroic confrontation with the chaotic to explore the inner chaos of Achilles' psyche, the poet of the *Iliad* has expanded the meaning of the mythic paradigm in a fascinating and provocative way. When the battle between the chaotic river and the fire of Hephaestus comes to symbolize an inner spiritual battle, we sense a profound paradox. While it is true that the fire of Hephaestus defeats the Scamander, fire, being an ambivalent symbol, also represents destructiveness. Thus two ambivalent symbols, put into irreconcilable conflict, express the all-consuming and annihilating powers of the chaotic. This symbolism means that for Achilles the same fire that defeats the Scamander will eventually consume him as well. The paradox is that Achilles' supra-human and divine invincibility with its putative immortality leads him ultimately to both the knowledge and experience of death. All the same, he is, at least for a time, invincible.

Liminality and Death

In both the *Gilgamesh Epic* and the *Iliad*, the mythic pattern of heroic conflict with chaos connects liminality and death. This is

reinforced in the scene where Thetis comes to console Achilles
over the death of Patroclus, and speaks to him of his own death:

ὠκύμορος δή μοι, τέκος, ἔσσεαι, οἷ᾽ ἀγορεύεις·
αὐτίκα γάρ τοι ἔπειτα μεθ᾽ Ἕκτορα πότμος
ἑτοῖμος. (18.95–96)

> *You will be quickly lost to me, my child, such are the*
> *words you speak: / your fated death is readied soon af-*
> *ter Hector's.*

Thetis' awareness that she will soon lose her son points to van
Gennep's ritual pattern whereby the liminal initiand is separated
from his mother and from the world of women and children in
general. He notes that invariably the moment comes when the
initiand is torn from his mother who weeps for him. It is not
unusual for this separation to be expressed in terms of funereal
preparations and death.[22] (Because the word ἑτοῖμος is more
appropriate to a *funeral* than *death*, πότμος, the collocation of
these two words reinforces the confused worry and grief of mother
Thetis.)

Such is the situation in the *Iliad* when Thetis comes to comfort Achilles as he is stretched out in a deathly pose, mourning
Patroclus, and having covered himself with dust (*Il.* 18.23–27).[23]
Thetis is accompanied by the other Nereids, and their appearance
suggests a funeral chorus bewailing Achilles as though he were
already dead (*Il.* 18.50–52). The significance, then, of this scene,
especially when seen in the light of van Gennep's pattern, is that
Achilles' isolation and liminality not only takes on the aspect of
death—his separation and alienation become akin to the final
isolation of death itself—it also reinforces the tragic perspective
whereby Achilles, Patroclus, and Hector are all linked by the same
destiny. It would not be amiss to observe at this point that a
frequent element in the stories of Greek tragic heroes and heroines
is their profound isolation.[24] At the same time, the necessary

attempt by the tragic poet to understand and put into perspective this tragic isolation results in various dramatic and literary ploys to minimize the hero's liminality and to suggest the ultimate reintegration that makes intelligible the entire tragic experience. To cite but three examples, Sophocles' *Antigone, Oedipus the King* and *Oedipus at Colonus* each have a tragic hero whose isolation increases in the course of the drama, and is a mark of the hero's tragic suffering. In *Oedipus at Colonus,* the poet ends Oedipus' liminality with an integrative apotheosis that makes intelligible his entire tragic career. In order to understand, in the case of Achilles, this strange, funereal scene with its premature lamentations by Thetis and the other sea nymphs, one must see it in relation to the *Iliad's* larger pattern, and especially in relation to Achilles' eventual reintegration into the society of his comrades.

Liminality and the Hero's Moral Status

Achilles' liminality is expressed through his heroic solitude, and is an integral part of his encounter with the chaotic. It also involves difficult moral issues, which the poet raises by having Achilles mutilate and maltreat the body of Hector, dragging it behind his chariot around the walls of Troy. Nagler well limns the difficulty many readers have with Achilles' brutality:

> It is not easy to understand Homer's Achilles against the vast backdrop that is achieved in this sometimes underrated section of the poem, except to say that his stature— for better or for worse—is great beyond the pale of ordinary comprehension. Myth at its most creative, of which the *Iliad* is an example, does not lend itself to one-sided evaluations of right and wrong; Achilles appears as the Promethean benefactor of mankind, the culture hero allied with natural powers such as fire to overcome nature's resistance and bring on the waters of fertility; but he also appears as the blocker of the waters, the bringer of death, hoarder, destroyer of social contracts and ultimately of the sacred boundaries between the living and the dead. Similarly, on the level of personal motivation,

> he is pictured as inconsistent and morally opaque, as
> perhaps no comparable character from the fiction of
> post-heroic ages.   His violent excesses are certainly
> repugnant to us.[25]

This natural perplexity can be addressed, at least in part, by
noting that Achilles, by virtue of his liminality, still stands outside
of the human community, and as such is not bound by its conventions. Van Gennep explains this social license:

> During the entire novitiate, the usual economic and legal
> ties are modified, sometimes broken altogether.   The
> novices are outside society, and society has no power
> over them, especially since they are actually sacred and
> holy, and therefore untouchable and dangerous, just as
> gods would be. Thus, although taboos, as negative rites,
> erect a barrier between the novices and society, the
> society is defenseless against the novices' undertakings.
> That is the explanation . . . for a fact that has been noted
> among a great many peoples and that has remained
> incomprehensible to observers. During the novitiate, the
> young people can steal and pillage at will or feed and
> adorn themselves at the expense of the community
> (*Rites of Passage*, 114).[26]

Another dimension of Achilles' uniqueness is his sacred nature: he is uniquely sacrosanct.[27] The moral ambivalence of his
status, whereby, like Prometheus or even more aptly, like Oedipus,
he is both a blessing and a curse, can be understood by the concept
of the "pivoting of the sacred," the term which van Gennep coined
to explain variation and change in the nature of the sacred. For
most primitive societies, the sacred is not absolute but relative: "it
is brought into play by the nature of the particular situations"
(*Rites of Passage*, 12). A particular individual may be sacred with
respect to one segment of society and not to another, and therefore
as he or she moves from one place or level to another, the sacred
or magic circle "pivots." Consequently, he who one day was sacred
may be the next profane, or vice-versa. In this way, the seemingly

incomprehensible brutality of Achilles becomes intelligible when one sees him as *sacer*, with the full ambiguity of that word.

Another way of understanding Achilles' ambiguous sacredness is along the lines suggested by Whitman in the first chapter of his *Heroic Paradox*.[28] At the heart of the heroic identity—that is, the way in which the hero sees himself in relation to the world at large—is the desire to become a god, or at least godlike. The quarrel with Agamemnon is the point at which the question of Achilles' heroic status together with the divine dimensions of that status comes into focus. Whitman writes:

> He asks for divine sanction upon individual heroism and upon his honor, but at the same time he dismisses his whole commitment to the Greek host, almost to humanity itself. Here is the individual asserting himself against society, in a way that threatens to make him no longer relevant to it. A man may assert his divine absolutism and thus in some sense 'become a god,' but then also after some fashion he ceases to be a human being, and he has no communication with anyone.[29]

Achilles' aspiration to divine status, that is, to the attributes of sacredness as he understands it, is closely connected to his rejection of his society's claims upon him. His unique sacredness makes him less human and more remote from human society, hence insensitive to its moral codes. Inasmuch as his behavior offends the moral sensibilities (and I think an ancient Greek audience would be no less offended than a modern one),[30] it is a mark of how far he stands outside of *all* human society. That is, his alienation from his fellow Achaeans at the beginning of the poem, through the course of events and especially through the death of Patroclus, has gradually been transmuted into a much more profound separation and alienation: in a very real sense, Achilles is no longer human. This is not to say that he is sub-human, nor by the same token, super-human. For to use these terms would be to pigeon-hole the unique status of the hero, when in point of fact he remains, as Homer intended, an enigma, transcending the conventionally intelligible boundaries that separate man from the gods on the one hand, and from the *infima species* on the other.

Reintegration

Achilles' liminal separation ends when he is at last reconciled with Agamemnon and restored to his companions. This reintegration comes about by the prominent role Achilles plays in the funeral games for Patroclus (he even gives Agamemnon a measure of recognition), and most especially by his nocturnal meeting with Priam, Hector's aged father, who has come to the Greek camp to ransom his son's body.

As part of the process of reintegration, Homer is concerned to portray his human qualities. To do this, he brings Achilles and Priam together in the poem's last book, where, in a scene of mutual recognition and regard, Achilles' reintegration reaches its natural fulfillment. Achilles' and Priam's discovery that they share a common bond of humanity is the means by which Achilles achieves his return to the society of his peers, and more importantly to the realm of humanity in general.

In his discussion of Vietnam veterans and their grief, Shay refers to the communalization of grief as an essential part of their recovery and return. He argues that PTSD, like other serious traumas such as the loss of a family member in a natural disaster, rape, exposure to mutilated victims of accidents, as well as combat, is ameliorated by the opportunity to talk about the traumatic experience, to give expression to the emotions felt at the time of the event, and to "experience the presence of socially connected others who will not let one go through it alone."[31] It seems that Homer has understood this necessity for his hero, but in order to emphasize the larger context of the human community in Achilles' movement from psychological chaos to social reintegration, he does not have the "communalization of grief" take place in the company of his Achaeans comrades, but with Priam, the aged Trojan king. It is, as many admiring critics have noted, a fine dramatic touch.

To identify the narrative elements that bring about Achilles' reintegration, there is first the theme of parenthood. Achilles' mother, Thetis, comes to him with the command to end his continuing mourning and the maltreatment of Hector's body (*Il.* 24.126–140). Of similar import is Hera's comparison of Hector and Achilles with specific reference to their mothers (24.58–60). Finally, Priam compares himself to Achilles' father:

μνῆσαι πατρὸς σοῖο, θεοῖς ἐπιείκελ' Ἀχιλλεῦ,
τηλίκου ὥς περ ἐγών, ὀλοῷ ἐπὶ γήραος οὐδῷ·
...
ἀλλ' αἰδεῖο θεούς, Ἀχιλεῦ, αὐτόν τ' ἐλέησον,
μνησάμενος σοῦ πατρός· ...(24.486–7, 503–4)

Remember your father, godlike Achilles, / who, the same age as I, is on the threshold of gloomy old age... But respect the gods, Achilles, and pity me, / remembering your father ...

And Achilles in turn:

ἀψάμενος δ' ἄρα χειρὸς ἀπώσατο ἦκα γέροντα.
τὼ δὲ μνησαμένω, ὁ μὲν Ἕκτορος ἀνδροφόνοιο
κλαῖ' ἀδινὰ προπάροιθε ποδῶν Ἀχιλῆος ἐλυσθείς,
αὐτὰρ Ἀχιλλεὺς κλαῖεν ἑὸν πατέρ', ἄλλοτε δ' αὖτε
Πάτροκλον· τῶν δὲ στοναχὴ κατὰ δώματ'
ὀρώρει. (24.508–12)

Taking his hand, he gently pushed the old man away. / And the two of them remembered; Priam, crouched before Achilles' feet, sobbed out loud for manslaughtering Hector, / and Achilles wept his own father, and again Patroclus. / The sounds of their grief filled the house.

It is clear, then, that parenthood, especially with its tragic aspects of separation and suffering, becomes a bond joining Priam and Achilles.

Another is food; Achilles says to the old king:

ἀλλ' ἄγε δὴ καὶ νῶϊ μεδώμεθα, δῖε γεραιέ,
σίτου· ἔπειτά κεν αὖτε φίλον παῖδα κλαίοισθα,
Ἴλιον εἰσαγαγών· πολυδάκρυτος δέ τοι ἔσται.
(24.618–20)

*But come now, we too, noble old man, must need think /
of food; henceforth you may mourn you dear son, / returning to Ilion, where your son will be much wept.*

Achilles' encouragement of Priam to eat, and his sharing a meal with him stands in contrast to his earlier refusal to eat, when his only concern was vengeance for the fallen Patroclus (19.303-8). Van Gennep has noted the importance of the rituals of eating and drinking, by which the initiand is reintegrated into his group or community:

The rites of eating and drinking together. . . is clearly a rite of incorporation, of physical union, and has been called a sacrament of communion. . . Often the sharing of meals is reciprocal, and there is thus an exchange of food which constitutes the confirmation of a bond. (*Rites of Passage*, 29)[32]

In addition to food, there is also the bond of sleep. Both Achilles and Priam sleep after their conversation (*Il.* 24.643–76). It is also significant that Achilles sleeps with Briseis; the suggestion of sexual union also betokens his return to human society. (The parallel to the humanization of Enkidu by the sacred prostitute in the *Gilgamesh Epic* is instructive.)

Achilles' reintegration not only reunites him with his fellow Achaeans, but it also, by virtue of the human commonalities he shares with Priam, symbolically rejoins him to the larger society of humankind as a whole.

Compensation

The issue of compensation is an important concern in the *Il-iad* and is connected to the theme of reintegration. As a solution to social crisis, ritual reintegration is often achieved through some compensatory action that reestablishes a sense of social order by the balancing of competing claims. As van Gennep explains, when the social group—be it family, village or clan—loses one of its productive members, some manner of compensation is required. Rites of passage and especially rites of separation, then, involve the "ransom" of something[33] as the form of compensation through which the ritual transition and the amelioration of social crisis are achieved.

The social crisis in the *Iliad* began with Agamemnon's de-mand to be compensated for his loss of Chriseis. Achilles expected compensation for his loss of honor, and then later for his loss of Patroclus. Finally, in the meeting of Achilles and Priam, the ancient king offers Achilles abundant ransom in compensation for Hector's body.

Both Achilles and Priam receive compensation for their re-spective losses, the deaths of Patroclus and Hector. In both cases, the acts of compensation facilitate the ritual passage from the realm of the living to the underworld. The poetic narrative under-scores the importance of these two transitional events, first by the appearance of Patroclus' ghost to remind Achilles to see to his funeral, and second by the elaborate description of Hector's funeral and the mourning of his fellow Trojans at the poem's conclusion. Thus, ritual acts of compensation lead to rituals of transition in the funerals of both Patroclus and Hector, which in turn point back to Achilles and his (ritual) reintegration into the society of his fellow Achaeans.

It is important to remember that Achilles is the focus of the epic, and that his symbolic kinship with Priam, set forth in the sharing of simple human experiences, points to the ultimate identity of their fates. Like Patroclus and Hector, both Achilles and Priam will one day make the transition from life to death, but for the present the important transition is the one which brings Achilles back into the sphere of his own companions, healing at last the isolation begun by his quarrel with Agamemnon in the first book.

Achilles' reintegration is also a process of restoring order after a confrontation with the chaotic. Compensation, ransom, and ritual transition are the means by which the return to social order is brought about. With Achilles' reintegration, therefore, we have come full circle from the military chaos occasioned by his quarrel with Agamemnon, his near psychological disintegration following Patroclus' death, and the life-threatening battle with the Scamander. As the poem continues its inexorable movement toward conclusion, we witness the resolution of the disorder both in the social realm, and most especially, in Achilles' own soul, as he becomes reconciled to his comrades and, symbolically at least in the scene with Priam, to his father.

Mourning: the Mythic Pattern of Niobe

Much of what has been said up to this point makes it clear that heroic confrontations with the chaotic are often expressed through ritual patterns. Ritual provides the mechanisms by which individuals and societies endeavor to confront the chaotic. Rituals of mourning are no exception. In the 24th book of the *Iliad*, Homer has Achilles tell Priam about Niobe and her endless mourning:

> ἡ δ' ἄρα σίτου μνήσατ', ἐπεὶ κάμε δάκρυ χέουσα.
> νῦν δέ που ἐν πέτρῃσιν, ἐν οὔρεσιν οἰοπόλοισιν,
> ἐν Σιπύλῳ, ὅθι φασὶ θεάων ἔμμεναι εὐνὰς
> νυμφάων, αἵ τ' ἀμφ' Ἀχελώϊον ἐρρώσαντο,
> ἔνθα λίθος περ ἐοῦσα θεῶν ἐκ κήδεα πέσσει.
> (24.613–617)

> 'Then [Niobe] remembered to eat, when she wearied of
> weeping. / But now, somewhere among the rocks, in the
> lonely mountains, / in Sipylus, where they say the god-
> dess nymphs have their beds, / and dance along the
> banks of the river Acheloios; / and there, though a rock
> still, she broods the sorrows given her by the gods.'

In telling Priam the story of Niobe, Achilles provides a mythic
paradigm for human grief and mourning. As she remembered to
eat, despite her suffering, so too Priam must eat despite his grief
for Hector. When Achilles tells how she was turned to stone in the
remote mountains of Sipylus, Niobe becomes, in his telling, a
universal mythic symbol of human grief.

In all of this, the most significant commonality shared by
Achilles and Priam is mourning. When he meets Priam, Achilles is
still mourning the loss of Patroclus, as Priam mourns the death of
Hector, and as earlier, Thetis mourned the anticipated death of
her son. This consistent pattern of mourning not only informs the
total movement of the *Iliad*, underscoring the ubiquitous sense of
war's tragedy, it also relates to the series of ritual transitions that
lie beneath the poem's narrative surface. For mourning, as van
Gennep maintained, is often an integral part of Rites of Passage.
Its cultural significance is that it provides a period of transition for
the survivors, who enter the period of mourning through rites of
separation, and end their mourning by rites of social reintegration.
Mourning also affords a symbolic link between the deceased and
the survivors: sometimes the transition period of the living is a
counterpart of the transitional period of the deceased, and the
termination of the first sometimes coincides with the termination
of the second; this means that the incorporation of the survivors
back into their society coincides with the incorporation of the
deceased into the world of the dead.[34] This parallelism is precisely
the form *Iliad* 24 employs with the two events of Achilles' reincorporation into human society and Hector's funeral in Troy.

There is also something paradoxical in this mythic picture of Niobe's grief. Though often expressed ritually as the response of a community to death, mourning is ultimately a solitary and liminal experience, as the stories of both Gilgamesh and Achilles make clear. So also with Niobe, who is placed among the remote rocks of Sipylus, in the lonely mountains of Asia Minor. Her isolated weeping is raised to something like a universal principle when she is depicted as a rock-face, ceaselessly dripping water from some hidden and unfailing spring. Her eternal mourning represents the universal and unchanging *lacrimae rerum* of human existence. Niobe is, as Kerenyi puts it, the "primordial image of man's fate, the endless dying of daughters and sons."[35]

When Achilles points out to Priam the relevance of Niobe's fate, we begin to sense the meaning she holds for him as well. His perspectives have so broadened that he now sees his own sorrows as part of the universal human tragedy expressed in the mythic image of Niobe.[36] In his ritual eating and drinking with Priam, in the funeral rituals, which now have increased importance for him, he sees himself and his own fate as part of a universal pattern. In this pattern, Achilles recognizes his kinship with Niobe no less than with Priam. This self-reflection and self-awareness are what lead to his rediscovered humanity.[37]

The stony weeping of Niobe, perhaps not unlike the wall of Uruk at the end of the *Gilgamesh Epic*, comes to symbolize Achilles' hard-won insights about death. His conflict with Scamander raised him beyond the human and mortal; his meeting with Priam not only returned him to the human, it also brought him to the point of appreciating the role of grief in human affairs, his own no less than Priam's. Achilles' insights about mourning, then, like other quotidian experiences of human life, underscore his return to the human realm. Where the death of Patroclus was the final event in the process of Achilles' separation from his social peers, now both his mourning for Patroclus and his prominent role in overseeing his funeral rites are (perhaps ironically) the first step in Achilles' reintegration. For Achilles' mourning initiates the chain of events that culminates in his meeting with Priam and his reintegration into humanity.

It is not surprising, moreover, that the mourning of Achilles and the mourning of Priam function in parallel ways. Achilles' mourning leads to his restoration, while the mourning of Priam not only motivates his journey to the Achaean camp, it leads to the ransoming of Hector's corpse and his proper funeral, both of which in turn will put an end to Priam's mourning. That Priam goes through something of a reintegration is made clear by the poet's narration of his return to Troy with its focus on the mourning of Hector's wife, Andromache, of the other Trojans, and even of Helen herself (24.710-end). Hermes, functioning as an agent of liminality, brings Priam back to Troy, where he immediately undertakes the preparations for Hector's funeral. Thus, we see clearly enacted the "transition period for the survivors," to use van Gennep's formulation.

All of these elements, then, that figure so prominently in the scene of Priam's meeting with Achilles, and especially the image of Niobe, function to bring Achilles back into the pale of human society where he can, as Whitman puts it,[38] "take part again in the ephemeral simplicities of the brief life which remains to him." At the same time, it should be emphasized that Achilles' return and reintegration, which is given expression by the pattern of movement from chaos to *cosmos*, also involve a new mythic and ritual awareness, a fuller understanding of life's sorrows as part of a universal pattern.

Conclusion

As one of the most puzzling episodes in the *Iliad*, Achilles' battle with the personified Scamander river gives vivid expression to the mythic idea of heroic conflict with chaos. In telling the story of his battle with this strange and powerful aquatic deity, the poet leads his audience to reflect upon the inner and external conflicts of his hero. The epic narrative looks both within and without—into Achilles' soul and the conflicts therein, where we see mirrored the upheavals and conflicts of the world without. Thus, the battle with the river comes to represent all those experiences that have led to his isolation and alienation.

The ritual expression of his isolation is liminality. Achilles' liminal nature leads him to contravene not only moral and social conventions but also his own psychological limits. So understood, Achilles' liminality represents the rupture of moral, social and psychological cohesion. In his battle with the Scamander, Achilles is so identified with his adversary that he becomes, on the one hand, a source of the chaotic, and, on the other, the force that restores order, symbolized by Hephaestus' fire. Thus, Achilles becomes, if I may so term it, a force for *cosmos*. Achilles' liminal isolation and its metaphysical tensions, when read in terms of his battle with the river, point to the chaotic as an essential character-istic of the heroic nature. In this way, the liminal and the chaotic come together to express the moral, psychological, and spiritual conflicts of a man who, in Whitman's words, is "too large for life."

Moreover, Achilles' movement into liminality and the chaotic leads inevitably to his death, but this movement also, paradoxi-cally enough, suggests his integration and eventual social whole-ness even in the face of death. For his experience of liminality and the chaotic leads to his acquiring a larger, more comprehensive understanding of what it means to be human. This is made clear by his words to Priam about the mourning of Niobe, who comes to be the mythic counterpart of Scamander. Both have connections with water, one a turbulent river, the other an ever-flowing moun-tain spring. I would argue, therefore, that these aquatic beings are universalizing mythic expressions of chaos and cosmos, the one consuming and annihilating, the other a source of healing and consoling. When, then, Achilles speaks to Priam about Niobe's mourning, he speaks as one who, through his encounters with the chaotic, has gained a much deeper understanding of the place of the chaotic at the core of human existence.

Notes to Chapter III

[1] Thomas Van Nortwick, Somewhere I Have Never Travelled: The Second Self and The Hero's Journey in Ancient Epic (New York: Oxford University Press, 1992), 40.

[2] Jonathan Shay, *Achilles in Vietnam: Combat Trauma and the Undoing of Character,* (New York: Atheneum, 1994), 5.

[3] Shay, ibid., 6.

[4] Shay, ibid., 10.

[5] Albert Lord, *The Singer of Tales* (Cambridge, Mass.: Harvard University, 1964) especially chapter 9.

[6] Michael Nagler, *Spontaneity and Tradition: A Study in the Oral Art of Homer* (Berkeley: University of California, 1974), chapter 5, "The Eternal Return in the Plot Structure of the *Iliad*," 131ff.

[7] Mary Louise Lord, "Withdrawal and Return: An Epic Story Pattern in the Homeric Hymn to Demeter and in the Homeric Poems," *Classical Journal* 62 (1967), 242–48.

[8] van Gennep, *Les Rites de Passage* (New York: Johnson Reprint Corporation, 1969), 13. Cf. also 279: Enfin la série des passages humains se relie même chez quelques peuples à celle des passages cosmiques, aux révolutions des planètes, aux phases de la lune. Et c'est là une idée gradiose de rattacher les étapes de la vie humainie à celles de la vie animale et végétale, puis, par une sorte de divination préscientifique, aux grands rythmes de l'univers.

[9] van Gennep, *The Rites of Passage*, tr. by Monika Vizedom and Gabrielle Caffee 189–90. Pour les groupes, comme pour les individus, vivre c'est sans cesse se désagréger et se reconstituer, changer d'état et de forme, mourir et renaître. C'est agir puis s'arrêter, attendre et se reposer, pour recommencer ensuite à agir, mais eutrement. Et toujours ce sont de nouveaux seuils à franchir, seuils de l'été ou de l'hiver, de la saison ou de l'année, du mois ou de la nuit; seuil de la naissance, de l'adolescence ou de l'âge mûr; seuil de la vieillesse; seuil de la mort; et seuil de l'autre vie-pour ceux qui y croient. (*Les Rites de Passage*, 272)

[10] James R. Redfield, *Nature and Culture in the Iliad*, expanded. (Durham: Duke University Press, 1994), 104–5.

[11] van Gennep, *Les Rites de Passage*, 161.

[12] For Achilles' ambiguous moral status, see the discussion regarding Achilles' moral status and the *pivoting of the sacred* (page 77).

[13] Gregory Nagy, *The Best of the Achaeans: Concepts of the Hero in Archaic Greek Poetry* (Baltimore: The John Hopkins University Press, 1979), 293.

[14] *Spontaneity and Tradition* (note 6 above), 149.

[15] *Spontaneity and Tradition* (note 6 above), 147. Other terms that he applies to the Scamander river are "chthonian monster, death god and chaos demon." In all of this Nagler sees the operation of an archetype, along the lines, it seems, of the Jungian archetypes of the collective unconscious. This archetype, moreover, involves no less than "the life and death of the race itself, the continued evolution of humankind, in a word destiny."

[16] See Cedric Whitman, "Fire and Other Elements," in *Homer and the Heroic Tradition* (Cambridge: Harvard University, 1958), 128–153.

[17] Cedric Whitman, *The Heroic Paradox: Essays on Homer, Sophocles, and Aristophanes* (Ithaca, New York: Cornell University, 1982), 20: "... we see him motivated by two simultaneous, opposite needs: the need for absolute status, and the need for human context, commitment; or, as the Greeks would put it, the urge toward divinity, and the necessity of remaining mortal. This is, one might say, the essence of the paradox."

[18] Shay, *Achilles in Vietnam* (note 2 above), 80. Cf. also his "Achilles: Paragon, Flawed Character, or Tragic Soldier Figure?," *Classical Bulletin*, 71 (1995), 119.

[19] Shay, *Achilles in Vietnam* (note 2 above), 82.

[20] Shay, ibid., 172.

[21] Shay, ibid., 173.

[22] *Les Rites de Passage* (note 8 above), 107.

[23] Shay, *Achilles in Vietnam* (note 2 above), 51, observes: "'I died in Vietnam' is a common utterance of our patients. Most viewed themselves as already dead at some point in their combat service, often after a close friend was killed."

[24] The lofty and austere isolation of Sophocles' Antigone comes to mind here.

[25] Nagler, *Spontaneity and Tradition* (note 6 above), 161.

[26] Pendant toute la durée du noviciat, les liens ordinaires, tant économiques que juridiques, sont modifiés, parfois même nettement rompus. Les novices sont hors la société ne peut rien sur eux et d'aut ant moins qu'ils sont proprement sacrés et saints, par suite intangibles, dangereux, tout commeseraient des dieux . En sorte que si d'une part, les tabous, en tant que rites négatifs, élèvent une barriére entre les novices et la société générale, de l'autre, celle-ci est sans défense contre les entreprises des novices. Ainsi s'explique, le plus simplement du monde, un fait qui a été relevé chez de très nombreuses populations et qui est resté incompréhensible aux observateurs. C'est que pendant le noviciat, les jeunes gens peuvent voler et piller tout à leur aise, ou se nourrir et s'orner aux dépens de la communauté. (*Les Rites de Passage,* 161)

[27] The sacred quality of Achilles is first suggested in the opening book of the epic by relationship between the hero and the seer Calchas. That is, it is Achilles who proposes consulting some seer (1.62), and it is to Achilles that Calchas directs his appeal for protection. Also, as Adam Parry pointed out (*H.S.C.P.* 76 [1972] 2), the way in which Agamemnon and Achilles are named in v. 7 makes clear the essential difference between them: Agamemnon is "lord of men" (ἄναξ ἀνδρῶν), while Achilles is "god-like" (δῖος); Agamemnon is defined by his position, Achilles by his nature.

[28] Note 17 above.

[29] *Heroic Paradox* (note 17 above), 25.

[30] For a good analysis of morality as it pertains to the behavior of characters in the *Iliad*, see Hugh Lloyd-Jones, *The Justice of Zeus,* 2nd ed. (Berkeley: University of California, 1983), 1–27.

[31] *Achilles in Vietnam* (note 2 above), 55.

[32] La commensalité, ou rite de manger et de boire ensemble. est nettement un rite d'agrégation, d'union proprement matérielle, ce qu'on a nommé un. Souvent la commensalité est alternative: il y a alors échange de vivres, ce qui constitue un lien renforcé. (*Le Rites de Passage,* 39–40)

33 *Les Rites de Passage* (note 8 above), 119.

34 *Les Rites de Passage* (note 8 above), 211.

35 Karl Kerényi, *Goddesses of Sun and Moon* (Irving, Texas: Spring Publications, 1979), 78.

36 See also Seth Schein, *The Mortal Hero: An Introduction to Homer's Iliad* (Berkeley: University of California Press, 1984), 162.

37 See Redfield's discussion of Achilles' "moralism," *Nature and Culture* (note 10 above), 217.

38 *Heroic Tradition* (note 16 above), 220.

�֍

Chapter IV
Odysseus and Poseidon

The Homecoming Theme

It is a commonplace that war changes people in profound ways. Returning soldiers find that the dehumanizing brutality of war and long absence have made the once familiar details of life at home strange and alien. Consequently, psychological distress, moral confusion, and spiritual dislocation often accompany postwar repatriation. In traditional Greek epic, songs of postwar return had become common in the singers' repertoire, and the names of a number of such homecomings or *nostoi* appear in the extant catalogues of early Greek epic.[1] Nevertheless, the only complete extant epic dealing with the *nostos* theme is Homer's *Odyssey*.

In telling the story of Odysseus' homecoming after ten years of war and another decade of wandering, the *Odyssey* develops the homecoming theme in such a way as to suggest that the hero's experiences are akin to rituals of passage. In addition, these ritual patterns in the *Odyssey* point to the phenomenon of psychological disintegration: in exploits that involve possible annihilation during his attempts to reach home and in his struggles once there to reclaim his wife and kingdom, Odysseus must repeatedly confront the question of what is real and what is merely the semblance of reality. Finally, all these experiences are connected with the larger mythic themes of chaos and order.

In support of these propositions, I would suggest that Homeric epic sees a parallel between the moral and political chaos caused by war in the external world and an analogous chaos in the warrior's psyche. In the *Iliad*, for example, the increasing intensity of the battles, especially as the Trojans approach the Achaean ships, anticipates Achilles' increasing martial fury later in the poem, culminating in his battle with the Scamander. This pattern of increasing brutalization and dehumanization in the poem's dramatic development suggests a movement into greater chaos. The *Odyssey* by contrast, in its portrayal of the painful rehumanization of a returning warrior, exhibits the reverse process, becoming, as it were, a humanizing antithesis to the earlier poem.

At the conclusion of hostilities, peace returns and warriors make their way home. Nevertheless, the returning soldier faces a difficult period of social, emotional, and psychological adjustment. The inner chaos of his soul, the result of his exposure to incessant brutality, must yield to an inner order more in harmony with the changed realities of the external world. To put it more broadly, the external chaos of war and the corresponding internal chaos of the warrior must both give way to a new order of things. Homer's *Odyssey* uses the homecoming theme to give dramatic focus to both of these dimensions of postwar life. To cite one telling example: Odysseus' failure to recognize Ithaca when left there by the Phaeacians (13.197–235) indicates the degree to which the hero and his perceptions have changed.

Ritual Passage and Poetic Structure

The *Odyssey*, then, develops homecoming into a multivalent and polytropic[2] metaphor for a soldier's transition from war to peace, from chaos to order; for Odysseus it is a transition from the Trojan war to the (anticipated) domestic tranquility of Ithaca. As a transitional experience, Odysseus' return to Ithaca can be expected to have metaphoric and conceptual affinities to the experiences van Gennep has identified with Rites of Passage.

In broad outline, the story of Odysseus corresponds to the pattern of ritual passage. The hero of the myth leaves his home and kingdom on the island of Ithaca in order to participate in the Greek expedition against Troy. The consequence of his lengthy absence is the dislocation and disjuncture of the island's political and social structure; when the poem opens, the crisis on Ithaca has come to a head with the incipient maturity of his son Telemachus, who presumably is soon to make his claim to the throne. For Odysseus himself, absence from Ithaca has meant a long period of *liminality*, both during his ten years as a warrior outside the walls of Troy and as an unknown vagabond for a second decade. Moreover, his long absence is responsible for the social crisis looming on Ithaca, and his liminal wandering provides the testing that will prepare him to return and rectify the long-standing social crisis in his homeland. During much of this time, he is in social limbo, outside the usual boundaries of civilized society. His process of reintegration begins with his departure from Calypso's island, progresses through a *rebirth* from the sea aided by Ino-Leucothea, and culminates in his return to Ithaca and reconciliation with faithful Penelope.

In his discussion of the usefulness of van Gennep's ritual pattern for analyzing Odysseus' return, Charles Segal[3] argues that Odysseus' journey from Troy to Ogygia, where he is held against his will by Calypso, represents a separation from his troops and his warrior past. His sojourn among the Phaeacians is primarily a "transitional situation," while his adventures on Ithaca represent his "reincorporation into the society he left behind, and fittingly culminate in a re-enactment of marriage." Segal concludes that "both the schema of the ritual and the structure of the poem share a common perception of a universal experience in human life."[4]

Similarly, Bruce Louden has discovered in the *Odyssey* "three sequences in a large-scale instance of ring composition."[5] The first sequence, comprising Books 1 through 4, focuses on Telemachus, the suitors, and Penelope. The second sequence begins when Odysseus encounters Poseidon on his way to Scheria, the land of the Phaeacians, and ends with the Phaeacian escort of Odysseus to Ithaca. The third sequence, comprising Books 9 through 12, is essentially the story Odysseus tells the Phaeacians about his wanderings. This is Louden's schema of the three sequences:

A1: Ithacan Sequence, Book 1 through Book 4
    B1: Scherian Sequence, end of Book 5.282 through Book 8
        C1: Aiaian Sequence: Book 9 through Book 11.332
            Intermezzo: 11.333–82
        C2: Aiaian Sequence: Book 11.383 through Book 12
    B2: Scherian Sequence, Book 13.1–187a
A2: Ithacan Sequence, Book 13.187b through Book 24.6

I would carry the analysis a step further by noting a correspondence in Louden's schema to the three-fold pattern of ritual passage. The theme of the first segment (A1) is the hero's separation and long absence from his home and his community on Ithaca. To be sure, the focus of Books 1 through 4 is the situation on Ithaca, yet the underlying interest of these books is Odysseus himself and what his absence has come to mean for his family and his kingdom. Although the traditional name of this section of the poem is the *Telemacheia* (the story of Telemachus), the real emphasis is the social and political chaos caused by the king's absence.

The second sequence (B1, B2) is the story of Odysseus' liminal wanderings. Book 5 opens with Athena expressing her concern to Zeus about Odysseus' fate; he responds by sending Hermes to Calypso to set in motion the beginnings of his return. Louden's second sequence ends with Odysseus' arrival on Ithaca. With the end of the second sequence (B2), the first sequence resumes, and details the events of his return, his political reintegration and restoration to his wife and throne (A2). Louden's third sequence (C1, C2), located at the center of the poem's ring structure, is the hero's Apologue, the story he tells the Phaeacians of his wanderings.

As is often the case with ring composition, the central section contains important emphases. This *intermezzo*, as Louden calls it, has Odysseus pause his story, and provides the Phaeacian king and queen an opportunity to comment on the storyteller himself, his narrative skills, and the veracity of his story. Their words clearly indicate this interpretative dimension. Queen Arete says:

Φαίηκες, πῶς ὔμμιν ἀνὴρ ὅδε φαίνεται εἶναι
εἶδός τε μέγεθός τε ἰδὲ φρένες ἔνδον ἐίσας;
(11.336–37)

Phaeacians, how does this man appear to you, with his good looks, his stature, and his well-balanced mind within?

In Arete's interpretation, handsome external appearances reveal the intelligence within. She invites the Phaeacians to share her appreciation of the understanding and wisdom Odysseus' liminal experiences have brought him. All the same, that she puts her observations in the form of a question suggests the larger issue: how can such fantastic tales of one-eyed cannibals, divine witches, and bags of winds persuade an audience as sophisticated as the Phaeacians? The Phaeacians, as well as Homer's audiences, and indeed modern readers of the poem could certainly question the literal truth of Odysseus' tale. By way of answer, Homer seems to indicate that Odysseus' words, like most mythic narratives, need to be read with a symbolic or metaphorical understanding. The poet himself points in this direction with the clever word play of king Alcinous himself, who, in asking about Odysseus' dead companions says:

ἀλλ' ἄγε μοι τόδε εἰπὲ καὶ ἀτρεκέως κατάλεξον,
εἴ τινας ἀντιθέων ἑτάρων ἴδες, οἵ τοι ἅμ' αὐτῷ
Ἴλιον εἰς ἅμ' ἕποντο καὶ αὐτοῦ πότμον ἐπέσπον.
νὺξ δ' ἥδε μάλα μακρὴ ἀθέσφατος· οὐδέ πω ὥρη
εὕδειν ἐν μεγάρῳ· σὺ δέ μοι λέγε θέσκελα ἔργα.
(11.370–74)

> *But come and tell me this truly, / if you saw any of your godlike companions, who followed you to Ilium and there met their doom. But this is a very long night, it is without end. It is not yet the hour for sleeping in the hall. But tell me your wondrous deeds.*

Two words here call for comment: ἀθέσφατος, which I've translated *without end*, simply seems to mean, on the one hand, *vast, immense, unending*, but, on the other, it also connotes *beyond even a god's power to express*, hence, *unutterable, unspeakable, awful* (LSJ). Although this adjective certainly refers to the long night of storytelling, its context, however, also suggests that the long night without end is Hades itself, and that Alcinous is also alluding to the *unending, unspeakable* terrors of the underworld. An eternity in Hades is the long, unspeakable night without end. The second word is θέσκελα (*marvelous, wondrous, awesome, set in motion by God*), which seems a semantic counterpart to ἀθέσφατος. Alcinous thus contrasts the immense eternity of Hades with the *wondrous* deeds of Odysseus himself. This contrast, moreover, lies at the heart of the *Odyssey*, whose hero ever struggles to find life in the midst of all the chaotic powers threatening to annihilate him. Alcinous' clever word play reveals his sophisticated appreciation of a storyteller whose incredible tales of *awesome* deeds in the *awful* recesses of Hades reveal profound truths about human nature and the human condition.

In this way, at the very center of the hero's story of his liminal experiences, the poet pauses the narrative to ask his audience to ponder not simply the literal meaning of the story, but the larger implications of the events being recounted. Moreover, the focus of this intermezzo on the storyteller himself suggests that the psychological consequences of his liminal experiences are no less important (cf. the discussion below, 112).

It can be argued, then, that the analyses of Segal and Louden indicate how van Gennep's ritual pattern can help interpret the poetic movement of the *Odyssey*. Although it may be debated whether Odysseus' liminality began with his original departure from Ithaca or his departure from Troy, the presence of liminal elements seems undeniable. Segal is very much on target in his perception of the significance of van Gennep's pattern:

> Deeply underlying these themes of transition is a basic mythical pattern fundamental to the epic of quest or search, namely the cyclical alternation of life and death; the rediscovery of 'life' after a period of sterility, darkness, imprisonment; the ultimate victory of life over death, of order over disorder.[7]

Odysseus' return marks the warrior's successful struggle against death and oblivion in an epic movement from death to life, from liminality to reintegration, from chaos to a new realization of psychological and political order.

Odysseus and the Sea

There are three occasions when Odysseus must confront a storm at sea: the first comes when he and his companions have sacked the city of the Cicones at Ismarus, and Zeus sends a fearsome storm:

> νηυσὶ δ' ἐπῶρσ' ἄνεμον Βορέην νεφεληγερέτα Ζεὺς
> λαίλαπι θεσπεσίῃ, σὺν δὲ νεφέεσσι κάλυψε
> γαῖαν ὁμοῦ καὶ πόντον· ὀρώρει δ' οὐρανόθεν νύξ.
> αἱ μὲν ἔπειτ' ἐφέροντ' ἐπικάρσιαι, ἱστία δέ σφιν
> τριχθά τε καὶ τετραχθὰ διέσχισεν ἲς ἀνέμοιο.
> (9.67–72)
>
> *Cloud-gathering Zeus drove Boreas, the north wind, against our ships / in a vast whirlwind, and the clouds hid from view / land and sea alike. Night sprang from heaven. / The ships were carried headlong, and the force of the wind / shredded their sails into three and four pieces.*

The language and imagery of this description recur when Odysseus tells of the gale that kept him from making a timely departure from the land of Helios, the sun god:

ὦρσεν ἔπι ζαῆν ἄνεμον νεφεληγερέτα Ζεὺς
λαίλαπι θεσπεσίῃ, σὺν δὲ νεφέεσσι κάλυψε
γαῖαν ὁμοῦ καὶ πόντον· ὀρώρει δ' οὐρανόθεν νύξ.
(12.313–315)

*Cloud-gathering Zeus set against us a gale-force wind /
in a vast whirlwind, and the clouds hid from view land
and sea alike. Night sprang from heaven.*

The second storm is sent by Zeus to punish Odysseus' companions for eating the sun god's cattle:

δὴ τότε κυανέην νεφέλην ἔστησε Κρονίων,
νηὸς ὕπερ γλαφυρῆς, ἤχλυσε δὲ πόντος ὑπ' αὐτῆς.
ἡ δὲ ἔθει οὐ μάλα πολλὸν ἐπὶ χρόνον· αἶψα γὰρ
ἦλθε
κεκληγὼς Ζέφυρος, μεγάλῃ σὺν λαίλαπι θύων,
ἱστοῦ δὲ προτόνους ἔρρξ' ἀνέμοιο θύελλα
ἀμφοτέρους· ἱστὸς δ' ὀπίσω πέσεν, ὅπλα τε
πάντα
εἰς ἄντλον κατέχυνθ'·

...

Ζεὺς δ' ἄμυδις βρόντησε καὶ ἔμβαλε νηὶ κεραυνόν·
ἡ δ' ἐλελίχθη πᾶσα Διὸς πληγεῖσα κεραυνῷ,
ἐν δὲ θεείου πλῆτο·... (12.405–411, 415–17)

*Then the son of Cronus fixed a steel-blue cloud / over
the hollow ship, and the sea grew dark beneath it. / The
ship sailed on, but only for a little while, as suddenly the
screaming west wind came, raging in a great whirlwind, / and the blast of the wind broke the forestays of
the mast, both of them; the mast crashed backwards
and all the rigging / collapsed into the ship's hold.*

...

At once Zeus thundered and hit the ship with a thunder-
bolt, / and she was spun about; struck by Zeus' bolt, /
and she was filled with the odor of sulphur.

The third storm is roused by Poseidon, which shatters the
hero's frail raft as he sails from Calypso's island:

"Ὡς εἰπὼν σύναγεν νεφέλας, ἐτάραξε δὲ πόντον
χερσὶ τρίαιναν ἑλών· πάσας δ᾽ ὀρόθυνεν ἀέλλας
παντοίων ἀνέμων, σὺν δὲ νεφέεσσι κάλυψε
γαῖαν ὁμοῦ καὶ πόντον· ὀρώρει δ᾽ οὐρανόθεν νύξ.
σὺν δ᾽ Εὖρός τε Νότος τ᾽ ἔπεσε Ζέφυρός τε δυσαὴς
καὶ Βορέης αἰθρηγενέτης, μέγα κῦμα κυλίνδρων.
...
                    ... ἔλασεν μέγα κῦμα κατ᾽ ἄκρης,
δεινὸν ἐπεσσύμενον, περὶ δὲ σχεδίην ἐλέλιξε.
τῆλε δ᾽ ἀπὸ σχεδίης αὐτὸς πέσε, πηδάλιον δὲ
ἐκ χειρῶν προέηκε· μέσον δέ οἱ ἱστὸν ἔαξε
δεινὴ μισγομένων ἀνέμων ἐλθοῦσα θύελλα,
τηλοῦ δὲ σπεῖρον καὶ ἐπίκριον ἔμπεσε πόντῳ.
(5.291–296, 313–318)

So [Poseidon] spoke, and gathered the clouds together
and roiled the sea / taking the trident in his hands. He
roused all the squalls / of the winds from all quarters,
and the clouds hid from view land and sea alike. Night
sprang from heaven. / Eurus the east wind, and Notus
the south wind, and Zephyr that blows trouble from the
west, / and Boreas, the aether-sprung north wind,
rolled up the heavy billowing waters.
...
*   A huge wave drove down from above / rush-*
ing on with terror, and spun the raft in a circle. / The
man himself was thrown far from the raft, / and
dropped the tiller from his hands.   Its mast was
snapped in two by the coming of a fearsome blast from
a jumble of winds. The sail and its yard fell into the sea
some distance away.

All three storms reveal parallels and suggest thematic coher-
ence.[8] Given the structure of the poem and the central importance

of the Apologue in the poem's narrative movement, I would suggest that the first and last of these storm narratives serve to frame Odysseus' liminal experiences. The first one is connected to the disastrous encounter with the Cicones, the first episode in Odysseus' story. The last one brings him to the land of the Phaeacians, the penultimate stop in his wanderings. This last storm differs from the rest in two important respects: it is narrated by the poet and thus falls outside the scope of the Apologue; it is also the first storm to be described in the poem and sets the pattern for the rest.

All three emphasize either Odysseus' separation from his companions or the solitary nature of his confrontations with the chaotic sea. It is perhaps of some significance that the first of the storms encountered and reported by Odysseus occurs in the context of the raid on the Cicones. Because this was a brutal act of sheer piracy and had disastrous consequences for Odysseus and his companions, its psychological impact on Odysseus is not insignificant and colors the rest of the Apologue (cf. e.g. his words of grief at 9.62–66). One hint of this psychological dimension is the change of the personal pronoun Odysseus uses in describing his departure from Ismarus. He consistently uses the first-person plural form of the verb to speak of himself and his companions until the point where he is driven off course by the forces of wave and wind. He then switches to the singular form to express his loss of homecoming:

> Καὶ νύ κεν ἀσκηθὴς ἱκόμην ἐς πατρίδα γαῖαν,
> ἀλλά με κῦμα ῥόος τε περιγνάμπτοντα Μάλειαν
> καὶ Βορέης ἀπέωσε, παρέπλαγξεν δὲ Κυθήρων.
> (9.79–81)

> *And now I would have arrived safe in my native land /*
> *as I rounded Maleia but the waves and the current /*
> *and the North Wind drove me past Cythera.*

This change in number suggests both his separation from his men and his awareness in retrospect of the losses to come. At this point, he has lost six men from each ship to the Cicones, and, as he tells his story to the Phaeacians, he cannot help but remember that he will lose more to Polyphemus and Scylla, and eventually his whole company in the storm off Thrinacia.

All three storms also paint a vivid picture of violent and chaotic nature. We note the liminal symbolism: Odysseus' ship and later his raft spin out of control; the hero finds it necessary to drop the tiller, thus losing any further hope of controlling the course of his vessel. The formulaic expression, σὺν δὲ νεφέεσσι κάλυψε / γαῖαν ὁμοῦ καὶ πόντον· ὀρώρει δ᾽ οὐρανόθεν νύξ, not only paints a vivid picture of turbulence and chaos, it also hints at the liminal confusion of one engulfed in it. Perhaps the one thing that sailors ancient and modern fear most is the loss of bearing. Ancient sailors, in particular, avoided losing sight of land, and feared cloudy nights without visible stars for navigation. This phrase, then, suggests the reaction and perspective of sailors caught in a storm at sea. Indeed, the very distinction between day and night is obscured: earth, sea, and sky become one chaotic shroud enveloping all the geographic features necessary for finding one's bearing. Similarly, the consequences of the liminal strife are brought out by the destruction of the vessel, and in particular, those parts of it that provide motion and direction. The mast is snapped in two: sails are shredded; the tiller is wrenched from his hands. The common element in all these descriptions, then, is the loss of one's bearings, the loss of control, and the sense of utter helplessness in the sea's violent onslaught.

In spite of the obvious elements of disorder and chaos in the description of Poseidon's violent sea, the phrase παντοίων ἀνέμων and the polysyndeton in the naming of the four winds (with the implicit contrast between the figure's emphasis on the individual winds and the explicit disorder of the scene) inject into the description a hint of tension between the elements of order and chaos. Not only do the winds come from the four points of the compass, the rolling swells of the sea's surface and its hidden currents (κῦμα ῥόος τε) suggest an implicit rhythm and order in the sea's chaotic violence. Poseidon also observes that his powers to destroy the hero are limited by fate, when he sees Odysseus approaching the Phaeacian coast, "where he is fated to escape the great test of woe that is coming" (ἔνθα οἱ αἶσα / ἐκφυγέειν μέγα πεῖραρ ὀϊζύος, ἥ μιν ἱκάνει). Odysseus' liminal testing will not destroy him: Poseidon's chaotic powers fall somewhat short of omnipotence.

All the same, Poseidon is an important presence in the _Odyssey_. In his study of the "extended narrative pattern in the Odyssey," Bruce Louden has seen in the poem's overall structure a thematically repeated emphasis on Poseidon's role in the story of Odysseus' travails.[9] Not only is he the cause of the shipwreck of Odysseus' frail raft in book 5, he reappears in book 13 to destroy the Phaeacian ship (13.162–64). Moreover, the formula κῦμα ῥόος τε tends to occur in connection with Poseidon as the specific agency by which his workings "are carried out," and as such are the touchstones of his hostility to the hero.[10]

It is also worth noting that Poseidon's hostility to Odysseus parallels the hostility of the Scamander to Achilles in the _Iliad_. Both gods would dearly love to destroy their respective adversaries, but are prevented by the intervention of other gods, and especially Hephaestus in the case of the river deity, and by Odysseus' fated homecoming. Moreover, the words κῦμα and ῥόος (in various combinations) are applied to both gods at the height of their violent actions.[11] These two words, then, especially when used in conjunction with one another, point to the presence of liminal ambiguity in the hero's plight.[12]

The Role of Calypso

Our first view of Odysseus himself comes at the beginning of the fifth book when Hermes is sent by Zeus to Calypso with the injunction that she must send him on his way to Ithaca. Calypso's island is described as a natural paradise with lush vegetation and an abundance of animals. Hermes does not find Odysseus with Calypso, but he is sitting alone on the beach, looking out over the vast expanse of the barren sea, breaking his heart in lamentation (5.82–84). When Hermes tells Calypso that she must send Odysseus on his way, she complains that the gods are hard-hearted and resentful when goddesses marry mortal men. She cites the fate of Orion, killed by Artemis because Dawn took him to bed, and the fate of Iasion killed by Zeus for mating with Demeter. Calypso's complaint of being deprived of a mortal mate echoes Ishtar's similar complaint when Gilgamesh refuses her offer of marriage. In spite of her resentment, Calypso promises to release Odysseus and "solicitously give him my advice, nor hold back, that he may arrive unharmed in his native land" (5.116–144).

Scholars have long noted that Calypso, like Circe, has a number of features in common with Near Eastern goddesses such as Siduri and Ishtar. Despite their lushness, her surroundings are, all the same, a liminal wilderness, and she, like the sacred prostitute in the *Gilgamesh Epic*, functions as an agent of liminality. Not only does she give Odysseus usufruct of her sexuality, she also teaches him about his future, at least to the extent of providing the knowledge necessary for his homecoming (even teaching him how to navigate by the stars, 5.272–77). She also helps him plan his journey (5.233), she gives him the tools he need to build the raft (5.234–237), she shows him where to find suitable lumber (5.237–41), and provides the cloth for its sail. Finally, she puts his provision on board the raft and calls forth a following wind (5.265–68). Like the sacred prostitute who humanizes Enkidu, Calypso's humanization of Odysseus takes the form of providing the tools

and resources he needs to return to the human world. The importance of this aspect is suggested by the detailed description of the
raft's construction. His skilled carpentry is the measure of his
human technology, and Calypso's aid in the work is part and
parcel of her role as an agent of liminality.

While he is with Calypso, Odysseus is in a liminal limbo; hidden and remote from the human world, its social structures and
communities, he suffers solitude and separation. In short, he
inhabits the interstices between the states of mortal and immortal,
between times of heroic wanderings and homecoming, between
almost total isolation and reintegration into human community.[13]

Rebirth as a Rite of Passage

To describe the beginnings of Odysseus' return and reintegration, Homer employs imagery drawn from the birth process.
Because birth is an occasion for ritual and is frequently accompanied by rites of passage, the imagery describing Odysseus' escape
from Poseidon's sea and his landing on Scheria is an important
element in his rebirth from liminal obscurity. Having made his
departure on a homemade raft from the oblivion of Calypso's
island (this goddess' name means *concealer*),[14] Odysseus is espied
by Poseidon, who sends a fearsome storm, shattering the frail
vessel. Only the intervention of the goddess Leucothea keeps
Odysseus from drowning, as he wraps himself in her divine veil
(κρήδεμνον)[15] to preserve his life (5.282–473). Holtsmark's
analysis of this episode as a spiritual rebirth makes clear that
Odysseus, not only when he is on Calypso's island, but also as he
struggles with Poseidon's angry sea, is outside the realm of civilized society.[16] In particular, he argues that the hero has encountered Death through a number of his experiences, and that the
final confrontation with Death is his enforced stay with Calypso.
To have remained with this dread goddess would have meant not
the eternal life she promised but eternal death. Instead, his

departure and his struggle on the sea take on the character of a spiritual rebirth. The specific points in Holtsmark's analysis are worth noting: the battering waves of Poseidon's storm are "the spasms of the labor of birth" (208); the hero's nakedness is the nakedness of the prenatal infant; the food-bearing raft represents "placental security." Leucothea's veil, which she gives to him to tie around his chest, and which he throws back into the sea upon reaching land, is "the umbilical cord that has sustained his life during the final stage in the womb"; and when he throws it into the sea, he severs "himself of all connections with his prenatal existence" (209–10). The ministrations of Athena are those of a midwife who helps at "the critical moment of birth" as she aids Odysseus' exit from the sea. The crust of salt, which covers the hero at his egress, is the "unsightly dross," the *vernix caseosa* "that still clings to him from his watery womb." Finally, Holtsmark argues that the covering of forest leaves with which the hero wraps himself to preserve the spark of life is the soft swaddling blanket in which the newborn infant is wrapped. All of these allusions to the birth process suggest spiritual rebirth, ultimately leading Odysseus home to Ithaca, where he will achieve "wholeness as an integrated human being in the real world" (210).

Odysseus' rebirth, then, marks both his return to civilized society and conceptualizes his return as ritual passage. As with all such passages, it involves considerable danger and terror. When Odysseus leaves Calypso's island, he leaves behind the safety and security of the womb to engage a world fraught with peril and risk.[17] For to be born is to confront the world's chaos. Homer suggests that a part of Odysseus' discovery of self is this lesson. In that strange dialogue with Penelope, in which he both conceals and reveals his identity, he speaks of her long absent husband:

καὶ γὰρ τὸν Κρήτηνδε κατήγαγεν ἲς ἀνέμοιο,
ἱέμενον Τροίηνδε παραπλάγξασα Μαλειῶν·
στῆσε δ' ἐν Ἀμνισῷ, ὅθι τε σπέος Εἰλειθυίης,

ἐν λιμέσιν χαλεποῖσι, μόγις δ' ὑπάλυξεν ἀέλλας.
(19.186–189)

*For the force of the wind drove him also to Crete, / as he
was hastening to Troy, and drove him from his course
past Maleia. / And so he dropped anchor at Amnisus,
where Eileithyia has her cave, in a difficult harbor, and
with difficulty did he avoid the wind's gales.*

In this reference to Eileithyia, the goddess of childbirth, the poet
has Odysseus refer to the sequence of events that brought him
from Calypso's cave through Poseidon's stormy sea to landfall and
rebirth on Scheria. Conventional etymology connects Eileithyia to
ἔρχομαι, ἐλεύσω*, *to come.* Thus, Odysseus' veiled words hint of
his difficult "coming forth" from the gale-tossed waves of the sea
to the tranquility of Phaeacia. These words also allude to Calypso
in her role as midwife to his rebirth, and signal the end of his
liminal wanderings. This language of ritual passage, therefore,
subtly reveals to Penelope both her husband's salvation and the
terminal limits of his liminal story.

Rituals of Death

In the midst of his struggles, the hero gives expression to desperate questions:

Ὤ μοι ἐγὼ δειλός, τί νύ μοι μήκιστα γένηται;
...
. . .νῦν μοι σῶς αἰπὺς ὄλεθρος.
τρισμάκαρες Δαναοὶ καὶ τετράκις, οἳ τότ' ὄλοντο
Τροίῃ ἐν εὐρείῃ, χάριν Ἀτρείδῃσι φέροντες.
ὡς δὴ ἐγώ γ' ὄφελον θανέειν καὶ πότμον ἐπισπεῖν
ἤματι τῷ ὅτε μοι πλεῖστοι χαλκήρεα δοῦρα
Τρῶες ἐπέρριψαν περὶ Πηλείωνι θανόντι.
τῷ κ' ἔλαχον κτερέων, καὶ μευ κλέος ἦγον Ἀχαιοί·
νῦν δέ με λευγαλέῳ θανάτῳ εἵμαρτο ἁλῶναι.
(5.299, 304–312)

> *Oh wretched man that I am! What now, at long last,*
> *befalls me? /*
>
> ...
>
> *Now my sheer destruction is certain. / Thrice and four*
> *times blessed were the Danaans who perished then / in*
> *broad Troy, conferring favor on the sons of Atreus. / If*
> *only I had died and found my doom / on that day when*
> *the Trojans in their numbers / hurled their bronze-fitted*
> *spears at me, / over the dead body of Peleus' son. / Then*
> *I would have obtained funeral honors and the Achaeans*
> *would have granted me glory. / But now I am fated to*
> *be caught in a wretched death.*

Anticipating certain death, Odysseus reflects on what now seems to him a preferable demise—perishing long ago at Troy. The language he uses, however, is tinged with a sardonic irony. The word αἰπύς has the literal sense of *steep, sheer*, and comes to mean "falling headlong" (not unlike the Latin *praeceps*), hence "quick" or "sudden." The word σῶς (σάος) involves a play on words: instead of the usual meaning "safe" or "secure," it here has the sense of "sure", "certain" "inevitable." Thus, the *safety* he so desperately needs becomes the *certainty* of his destruction. Odysseus also utters the sardonic observation about others who died at Troy, "conferring favor on the sons of Atreus." The idea seems to be that the Atreidae would feel a measure of gratitude toward these dead for their sacrifice in a worthy cause, which seems a contrast to the meaningless death he now finds himself contemplating.[18] Similarly, Odysseus believes that death in Troy would have involved funeral rituals with their attendant honors and glory (κλέος). Instead, he now envisions only the oblivion of an unheralded, unknown, and unmourned death in the depths of a chaotic sea. In terms, then, of ritual passage, Odysseus mourns his loss of funeral rites as well as the oblivion of dying unknown and unhonored.

Common to all of the storm episodes in the *Odyssey* is the sense of loss of control, of helplessness in the midst of chaotic violence. Implicit also in all of them is the presence of impending death, perhaps the most fearsome part of liminal chaos. Odysseus' reflections, therefore, not only reveal his terror, they also suggest his political, social, and emotional perspectives on dying. The allusion to the death of Achilles, moreover, explicitly connects Odysseus and Achilles by the commonality of the theme of heroic death. Psychologically, Odysseus is thrown back to a recollection of the most traumatic event for the Achaeans in the whole of the Trojan war—the death of their greatest warrior—and uses the language of ritual passage to express his own terror at the prospect of dying.

The Psychology of Terror

Because the sea in mythic thought often represents the chaotic,[19] Poseidon's attempt to superinundate Odysseus also comes to represent all the forces of annihilation that threaten the well-being of the returning hero. Every warrior in his own way must make the difficult return, a return at once fraught with social, political, and psychological dangers. Not only does his struggle with Poseidon's angry sea and subsequent shipwreck become a poetic image of man's struggle with the chaotic powers of nature, it also expresses political, social, and psychological chaos.

Greek mythic epic, as it so often does, represents inner fears and terrors through anthropomorphic gods. Poseidon's words, when he catches sight of Odysseus, seem particularly apt for this psychological dimension: ἀλλ' ἔτι μέν μίν φημι ἄδην ἐλάαν κακότητος (5.290). (*"But still I purpose to drive him to a satiety of evil."*) Not only does this "satiety of evil" (ἄδην κακότητος) point both to the hero's shipwreck and his internal psychological turmoil, it also echoes the Iliadic formula "satiety of war" (ἄδην πολέμοιο) at *Il.* 13.315 and 19.423. (Both phrases in their specific contexts, it should be observed, contain a note of sardonic sarcasm.)

This psychological dimension first comes to the fore in the poem when, in the midst of Poseidon's storm, the poet describes its effect on Odysseus, using the traditional formula for physical and mental collapse: καὶ τότ' Ὀδυσσῆος λύτο γούνατα καὶ φίλον ἦτορ, 5.297. ("*And then Odysseus' knees and dear heart went slack.*") The confrontation with his chaotic adversary, in the first moments of their meeting, completely undoes Odysseus, both physically and psychologically. In attempting to grasp the nuances of the difficult phrase φίλον ἦτορ, I would suggest that it connotes a certain inner confidence and sure sense of self. (Lattimore translates it *inward heart*.) It is, then, roughly equivalent to Vergil's *conscia virtus* (applied to Turnus' long delayed realization of his true plight, *Aeneid* 12.668). Its loss, then, in the face of Poseidon's storm, would be the rush of adrenalin along with the sudden shock of realizing that death is unavoidable and imminent. Only by starts does Odysseus return to himself and begin to assert his will to survive: he moves for safety to the center of the raft, where he hopes to find some measure of protection.

It can be argued that Poseidon's *satiety of evil* and the formulaic response of the hero's knees and heart are intended to recall all the horrors of war and their psychological effect upon the combatants. In his study of Post Traumatic Stress Disorder (PTSD), Jonathan Shay notes the almost universal experience of Vietnam veterans suffering from PTSD: a horror beyond description, not only by reason of the brutalities that war necessarily imposes, but also because of the sense of moral betrayal and violation. Returning Vietnam veterans brought back with them memories of experiences beyond description and beyond understanding.[20] The poet of the *Odyssey*, in this pivotal encounter between his hero and the chaotic god of the sea, has Odysseus remember the horrors of battle before the wall of Troy, and uses this recollection to point to the physical and psychological consequences of war in the context of the larger pattern of the warrior's struggle for *nostos*. In his attempt to capture something of an experience beyond description, the poet narrates the story of one hero's attempt to return home, who nevertheless finds himself in a world that is strange and alien, a world beyond the limits of ordinary human reality, a world in which the usual standards of human behavior simply do not exist.[21] Shay describes the psychological effects of war upon the mind and perceptions of soldiers:

> Danger of death and mutilation is the pervading medium of combat. It is a viscous liquid in which everything looks strangely refracted and moves about in odd ways, a powerful corrosive that breaks down many fixed contours of perception and utterly dissolves others.[22]

It is important to distinguish between war's reality and its strange refractions in the mind of the soldier. The *Iliad* dealt with its reality (at least in part), the poet of the *Odyssey* is more concerned with its lingering effects in the psyche of his hero. As Odysseus struggles to realize his *nostos*, he must confront this alien and chaotic world, move through it, and by dint of physical and mental exertion return to the rational and real world he left years before. The hero of the *Odyssey*, especially as he confronts monsters, witches and strange divinities, suffers from a form of PTSD, and the poet seeks to give expression to the terrors of that experience through the various episodes of his hero's return. This dimension of the poetic narrative explains in part the dreamlike quality of Odysseus' remembered and narrated experiences, especially before the Phaeacians, but also on Ithaca. The fairy-tale world of his experiences—and even the trip to Hades—is akin to the dreams recalled, analyzed, and explained in traditional psychotherapy. Odysseus' Apologue is not simply a story to entertain the Phaeacian court, but a form of therapy, by which he sorts out in his own mind the meaning of his dreams and the reality of the experiences that lie behind them. Even the very land of the Phaeacians has a dream-like quality: its mountains are covered in shadows, ὄρεα σκιόεντα, (5.279), and it resembles a shield lying in the mists of the sea, ῥινὸν ἐν ἠεροείδει πόντῳ (5.281). It can be argued, then, that Phaeacia comes to represent that misty place in Odysseus' recollections where dreams and reality intersect. [23]

> [The poet of the *Odyssey*] takes his listener into a mythi-
> cal world of dreams, but it is a mirror image of the real
> world, where there is want and grief, terror and suffer-
> ing, and where man is helpless.[24]

By using the language of ritual passage, the poet of the *Odys-sey* invests his hero's transitions from one ritual stage to another with broad symbolic implications, the most important of which seem to play out on a psychological level. Odysseus' departure from the enchanting, but also dead-end tranquility of Calypso's island, is the juncture of his liminal and reintegrative stages. Not only is it the point where he begins his return to human commu-nity, it is also the point where he begins the return to self, that is, to a new understanding of himself and his place in the world.

Where the *Iliad* describes the terrors of war and their effect on warriors, the *Odyssey* limns the ways in which the hero, by recounting and thus re-experiencing those terrors, finds healing and return. Poetically, this healing comes both through the hero's narration of his adventures, and the recognitions that reveal him to the various audiences of his tales, and, no less importantly, to himself as well.

The intersection of dreams and reality is also a place of suffer-ing. The place of healing is also a place of pain. By making the connection between the very meaning of Odysseus' name and suffering, Dimock also suggests the inevitable connection between pain and human existence:

> There is no human identity in other terms than pain... To
> see life in any other way is to live in a dream world, as
> the Cyclopes do, and the Phaeacians...both are out of
> touch with reality.[25]

Over and against that real pain is the dreamworld of both the
Cyclopes and the Phaeacians. Throughout the poem, there is an
on-going tension between reality and unreality, often taking the
form of an implicit question: what is real and what is only the
semblance of reality? This tension reaches its culmination on
Ithaca when the island's true king arrives in the guise of a home-
less beggar. I would be inclined to argue, then, that both the
stories Odysseus tells the Phaeacians and those he tells on Ithaca,
like the dreams and nightmares recounted by a PTSD soldier,
convey the reality of his experiences, but in a way that does more
concealing than revealing. The whole of his battle experiences are
recalled, but in a form transmuted by the passage of time and the
inevitable processes of repression. Not only is it true that the
Cyclopes and Phaeacians live in a dream world, they also inhabit
the dream world of the poem's long-suffering hero.[26]

Heroic Identity

The success of a warrior's transition from a world of war to a
world of peace depends upon his mental and psychological resources. To rediscover his sense of self, then, it is necessary for
Odysseus to disentangle the real from its semblance, and, what is
more important, to reestablish his heroic identity. That his heroic
identity is involved in his transition from the military to the
civilian world and in the related liminal pattern becomes clear
when one recalls the reason for Poseidon's anger. Poseidon's
anger is not so much the consequence of the blinding of Polyphemus—after all, the savage cannibal had it coming—but the hero's
boastful revelation of his name. Despite his companions' efforts to
check his egoistic words, Odysseus calls out:

> Κύκλωψ, αἴ κέν τίς σε καταθνητῶν ἀνθρώπων
> ὀφθαλμοῦ εἴρηται ἀεικελίην ἀλαωτύν,
> φάσθαι Ὀδυσσῆα πτολιπόρθιον ἐξαλαῶσαι,
> υἱὸν Λαέρτεω, Ἰθάκῃ ἔνι οἰκί᾽ ἔχοντα. (9.502–05)

> *Cyclops, if any mortal man should ask / of your eye's unseemly blindness, / say that Odysseus, sacker of cities blinded you, / son of Laertes, who has his home on Ithaca.*

Odysseus' stratagem of calling himself "Nobody" (Οὖτις), and then shouting his name and lineage when presumably safe beyond the monster's reach, not only reveals his identity, it also provides Polyphemus a means to avenge his blinding. Now knowing his tormentor's name, he can call down the wrath of his father, Poseidon. Behind this lies the idea that the knowledge of a person's name confers power over him.[27]

In his often-cited essay on the name of Odysseus, Dimock argues that Odysseus' act of shouting his name to the monster's face is an act of defiance, an act of deliberate self-exposure in order to be "somebody rather than nobody." In so doing, Odysseus confronts "the hostility of the universe," and challenges nature to do her worst in order to demonstrate "her ultimate impotence to crush human identity."[28] I would argue, however, that his adversary is not a savage nature, blind in her "indiscriminate blows," but the chaos of the world at large, represented by Polyphemus and especially his father Poseidon. Hence, his cry of defiance sets his identity over and against the chaotic powers of the universe. In challenging the liminal chaos of Poseidon's sea, he also challenges the whole liminal world he has experienced up to this point. This confrontation implicitly involves his attempt to understand its meaning for himself and his relationship to it. His defiance, therefore, brings with it a measure of meaning; it is an attempt to find a modicum of intelligibility in the powers he defies. Insofar as the chaotic forces of Poseidon's sea do not kill him, Odysseus is able to establish a limit to those very powers. He is, in a very real sense, about to impose a measure of order in the very realm of chaos. (This interpretation is suggested by the measured description of Odysseus' response to the swamping of his raft: he swims back to it, lays hold of it, and crouches down in its middle, "escaping death's end," 5.325–26).

Dimock's article points in this direction in two important ways. First, he notes: "to pass from the darkness of the cave into the light, to pass from being 'nobody' to having a name, is to be born." This existential coming to be—perhaps not unlike the big bang of modern cosmologists—sets in motion a whole series of events that will amplify the meaningfulness, not only of the newly born, but the whole of the cosmos as well. This coming to birth (φῦσις, to use an etymologically appropriate Greek term) is not unique to Odysseus, but belongs to every individual who comes forth from the chaotic darkness to claim his or her own unique identity. Hence, Odysseus' movement from *nobody* to *somebody* is also a movement from *nobody* to *everybody*, and his struggle to establish his identity in a hostile cosmos is the universal struggle of every human being.

Secondly, Dimock also calls attention to the imagery of shipbuilding that informs the description of Polyphemus' blinding:

> The hero's colonizing eye as he approaches the Cyclopes' [land], the remark that they have no ships or shipwrights, the shipbuilding technique employed in blinding Polyphemus and the mention of axe, adze and auger, the tools which enabled Odysseus to leave Calypso and set sail on his raft...[29]

On the one hand, this imagery sets Odysseus as a man of *techne*—the very hallmark of civilization—in opposition to the savage barbarism of the uncivilized Cyclopes.[30] On the other hand, it also establishes shipbuilding and the attendant act of seafaring as a potent symbol for confronting the savage chaos of the world by the application of reason and intelligence, that is to say, by imposing order on the chaotic.

The opposition of barbarism and civilization is also expressed through the theme of hospitality. With every new arrival in a strange land, Odysseus asks the same question, "whether they are savage and violent, and without justice, / or hospitable to strangers and with minds that are godly" (9.175–76 *et passim*). Steve Reece argues that in the Polyphemus episode Homer uses a parody of the hospitality theme by having Polyphemus *pervert* it with his comment about giving Odysseus the "guest-gift" of being eaten after the rest of his companions.[31] Because rituals of hospitality can be subsumed under the rubric of rituals of incorporation, Odysseus' expectation of traditional hospitality from Polyphemus and others points to the end of his liminality. With each new landfall, he looks for the signs of civilization that portend his homecoming. Polyphemus' claim not to fear the gods clearly places him beyond the borders of civilization, and puts his cave, like the Cyclopean lands in general, in the realm of liminality. Like Humbaba in the *Gilgamesh Epic*, Polyphemus is a liminal creature, violent and chaotic.

Thus, Odysseus' boastful self-identification ironically leads to his potential destruction, and significantly, from this point on, the hero is reluctant to reveal his identity, even concealing it from faithful Penelope. The essence of the hero, then, is his identity, and its importance for his position in the world is what leads to Poseidon's anger; but it is also the key to Odysseus' success and victory. That the question of Odysseus' identity is central to the story of his struggle with the sea is clear from the way in which it is framed first by his "almost total lack of self-identity"[32] on Calypso's island, and then by his bold claim of heroic identity at the court of the Phaeacians:

> εἴμ᾽ Ὀδυσεὺς Λαερτιάδης, ὃς πᾶσι δόλοισιν
> ἀνθρώποισι μέλω, καί μευ κλέος οὐρανὸν ἵκει.
> (9.19–20)

> *I am Odysseus, son of Laertes, known for my wiles / by all men, and my fame goes up to heaven.*

    Between these two points in the poem's movement, Odysseus confronts the chaos of Poseidon's angry sea, and realizes a ritual-like rebirth. This movement from seaborne annihilation to landfall and rebirth, in short, from chaos to renewal, establishes his heroic identity for those who hear his tale. No less important is Odysseus' self-recognition, that is, "the sense of one's own existence," to use Dimock's suggestive words. I would take the idea a step further and suggest that this sense of self also involves the idea of wrestling order out of chaos. Odysseus' understanding of his place in the world and the meaning of his existence issue directly from his confronting the chaotic nothingness of personal annihilation, which he saw before him in the angry waves of the sea. Working through that experience led him to the existential claim, "I am, I have a name, and that makes the world a different place, more orderly, and more intelligible than it would have been had I died."

    This emphasis on Odysseus' heroic identity can be compared to the portrayal of Achilles in the *Iliad*. Where the *Iliad* sets Achilles' will to divinity in opposition to the chaotic powers of the Scamander, the *Odyssey* sets its hero's self-identity against the world's chaos. In the earlier epic, the hero confronts the chaotic with his impulse to be more than human; in the *Odyssey,* it is the fundamental humanity of the hero that both defines his self-identity and impels him into conflict with the chaotic god of the sea.

    Odysseus' reborn humanity, therefore, with its characteristic abilities of reason and thought, places him in the role of one who creates things of order and structure. (His building of the raft on Calypso's island, to which the poet devotes a lengthy description, 5.234–61, suggestively anticipates this role.) Likewise, when he appears before the Phaeacian assembly, he tells the tale of his wanderings with such eloquence and grace that King Alcinous compares him to a singer:

σοὶ δ' ἔπι μὲν μορφὴ ἐπέων, ἔνι δὲ φρένες ἐσθλαί,
μῦθον δ' ὡς ὅτ' ἀοιδὸς ἐπισταμένως κατέλεξας,
πάντων τ' Ἀργείων σέο τ' αὐτοῦ κήδεα λυγρά.
(11.367–9)

*There is a graceful shape to your words and good sense
within, / so skillfully, like a bard, have you told the
story / of the grievous sorrows of yourself and all the
Argives.*

Like an epic singer (ἀοιδός), Odysseus is master of the civilized arts of poetry and song; with these, he is able to organize an orderly account of his experiences. His words have grace and structure: the word μορφή, traditionally translated *grace*, has the primary sense of *form* or *shape*, and in the present context suggests the orderliness of clear thinking (φρένες ἐσθλαί). In a similar way, by returning to Ithaca, and by putting an end to the depredations of the barbaric and chaotic suitors, Odysseus will restore political order and structure to his kingdom, taking his rightful place in its cultural and political affairs. Life therefore, in the fullest sense of creating order and meaning, has come from the sea through the rebirth of Odysseus.

Reintegration: The Meaning of Ino-Leucothea

An important mythological element in Odysseus' escape from Poseidon's chaotic sea is the goddess Ino-Leucothea, who, in a theriomorphic epiphany as the bird called "sea-crow,"[33] pities the hero's suffering, and reveals to him that Poseidon, in spite of his anger, will not destroy him. She also gives him her veil and tells him to tie it about his waist to effect his salvation from the sea.

While much could be said about the myth(s) of Ino-Leucothea,[34] it will suffice to consider only those elements that seem important to the story of Odysseus' salvation. The first is the apotheosis of Ino-Leucothea into a marine divinity. Pursued by enemies, or driven insane by Hera according to other versions, Ino

threw herself from a lofty cliff into the sea. Miraculously transformed into a goddess, she found salvation and deification instead
of death. This myth, perhaps originally connected to an act of
ritual sacrifice by immersion,[35] and possibly related to the primordial worship of the *Magna Mater*,[36] inverts the fate of Ino.
Not only is she deified into a sea goddess, Leucothea, she also
becomes a source of salvation to others, in particular sailors facing
annihilation in seaborne storms. The ritual mechanism involved
is identification. The prayers of fearful sailors would say in effect:
"you were threatened by death in the sea, yet you won salvation;
confer the same boon upon us."

With this intervention of Ino-Leucothea, therefore, Odysseus'
rebirth now takes on characteristics of apotheosis. The goddess
has the power to confer a salvation akin to immortality. The focus
of this gift centers on the immortal[37] and life-giving veil she offers
the hero. Being immortal, it has the implicit power to confer
immortality; she says to Odysseus: "there is no need for you to
suffer, nor to perish" (5.347).

Although the veil of Ino-Leucothea is the means by which the
goddess confers salvation upon the hero, it also symbolizes, as
Holtsmark has shown, the life-giving umbilicus. When interpreted
on this level, the symbolic relation between the hero and the
goddess becomes that of mother and son. It is significant that in
most forms of the Ino-Leucothea mythologem, the woman who
plunges into the sea is sometimes accompanied by a brother or
son. If the identification of the veil as umbilicus is valid (as the
multifold birth imagery suggests), Odysseus himself becomes the
goddess' son. This identification, moreover, is part of a larger
mythic pattern: the heroic son aided and supported by his goddess
mother.[38] One thinks of Achilles and Thetis, Aeneas and Venus,
and especially in the *Odyssey*, the hero's continuing and multifac-
eted connections with Athena.[39] The hero's salvation in this

mythic pattern, indeed his very status as hero, depends upon the intervention and aid of the divine mother figure.[40]

In his discussion of the experience of Vietnam veterans, Jonathan Shay draws a parallel between the role of Thetis in the *Iliad*, consoling her son Achilles in the midst of the terrors of war, and the "imaginary companion" that has sustained many soldiers (and others) in times of extreme danger and deprivation:

> One veteran in our program conversed regularly with a guardian angel while on long-range patrol in enemy territory. These dialogues became part of the shared life of his team, with his men asking him what the angel had said.[41]

Shay observes that such companions, angels, or personal patron saints "function as dramatized embodiments of combat soldiers' inner experience." It is a commonplace of Homeric studies that the gods often function as a poetic externalization of inner realities, specifically the cognitive and affective state of the poem's protagonist. Shay's observation of similar experiences by Vietnam veterans suggests a psychological explanation in that such experiences enable the soldiers to maintain psychic equilibrium in situations threatening physical and psychological annihilation. Read in this way, Ino-Leucothea serves to put the hero in touch with the inner psychic resources he must use to realize his salvation.

It is also possible to see Ino-Leucothea as an agent of liminality. Her role parallels that of Hermes, himself a liminal figure, who, earlier in the poem, persuaded Calypso to release Odysseus, and provided him with the magical *moly* for protection against the powers of Circe. Both deities abet the hero's transitional movement. So also Ino-Leucothea, who in the symbolic role of midwife,[42] aids the liminal hero as he moves from the chaotic realm of Poseidon's sea to the stability of Phaeacia. (We note the parallel to Siduri the barmaid in the *Gilgamesh Epic* when she advises that

liminal hero in his crossing of the sea to the land of Utnapishtim.)
Moreover Ino-Leucothea is also the agent of liminality for another
greater transition, the transition from death to life, as is suggested
by the umbilicus-like nature of her salvific veil.[43]

All of this means, then, that the kind of salvation involved in
Odysseus' escape from the sea is not merely physical survival, not
merely living through the shipwreck, but rather a kind of apotheosis similar to that of the goddess herself. The life-giving veil of
Ino-Leucothea, the symbolic umbilicus of his rebirth, not only
saves his life, it is also the means of his rebirth into humanity. In
this, there is a touch of ironic reversal: his refusal of Calypso's
immortality and his departure from her island leads to his rescue
and his homoeopathic apotheosis through the ministrations of
Ino-Leucothea. Odysseus' metaphorical apotheosis refers chiefly
to his salvation and rebirth; it is also the mythic equivalent of his
psychic and social reintegration into human community as reborn
hero.[44]

Every heroic encounter with the chaotic thus far considered
has, either explicitly or implicitly, had something to do with the
human aspiration to be more than human, i.e., to escape the bonds
of mortality. For Odysseus, his explicit refusal of Calypso's immortality led to his departure from her island, shipwreck, and
finally salvation by Ino-Leucothea, with its subtle hint of apotheosis. This seems to suggest that just as the hero cannot escape his
mortality and must eventually die, so also he cannot escape
immortality either. In this way, the mythologem of conflict with
the chaotic has at its very core a guarantee of inevitable immortality, either as a boon from a divine mother figure (Ishtar, Thetis,
Athena, Ino-Leucothea), or even, more prosaically, an immortality
acquired through fame and the notice of posterity. In any case,
Odysseus' rescue from the sea seems integral to the mythic pattern
of heroic conflict with the chaotic, and invests the pattern with
implications that go to the heart of the human condition.

Also implicit in the story of Ino-Leucothea is the theme of madness. Several versions of the myth report that Ino was driven insane by Hera, which led to her precipitous leap into the sea. There are also suggestions of madness in the non-Homeric mythic traditions connected to Odysseus: when the Greek heroes visited Ithaca in order to recruit him for the war, Odysseus feigned madness in order to avoid being compelled to join the expedition.[45] Hence, the themes of madness and potential destruction form the mythic background to the hero's salvation by Ino-Leucothea; and his successful return, no less than his salvation by the deified victim of madness, represents, on the psychological level, his escape from psychic annihilation. Not only does he escape the oblivion of Calypso' island and the inundation of Poseidon's sea, he also avoids the personal and psychic dislocation of the returning warrior. Thus, Ino-Leucothea represents psychic integration (externalized as apotheosis), just as Poseidon symbolizes psychic disintegration (externalized as shipwreck). Like Ino-Leucothea, who in a fit of divinely inspired madness threw herself into the sea, Odysseus too, madly rejecting Calypso's offer of immortality (on the face of it, incomprehensible folly), trusts himself to Poseidon's chaotic sea with only a fragile raft for safety. His transition, his rite of passage from the liminality of the warrior to reintegration as hero and king is successful because he survives, and because he avoids psychic disintegration.

Conclusion

As Achilles' struggle with the Scamander dramatized his quest for heroic and divine status, so also in the *Odyssey* the issue of human mortality lies in the background of the hero's struggle with the sea. When Calypso offers Odysseus immortality in order to entice him to remain with her, he refuses with the explanation that although both the goddess and her offer are attractive indeed, life with Penelope is his only desire.

Although the functional and sexual parallel between the sacred prostitute in the *Gilgamesh Epic* and Calypso in the *Odyssey*
suggests the presence of the *hieros gamos* pattern, Odysseus'
refusal of Calypso's offer is also the refusal of the sacralized
sexuality that ancient near-eastern goddesses were wont to prof-
fer. Nevertheless, Odysseus' experiences with this goddess, like
those of Enkidu, further his movement from liminality to reintegration.

In choosing to leave Calypso, Odysseus also chooses to confront the chaotic. Not only is Poseidon's sea a personification of
chaos, it also comes to represent evil.[46] This personified evil,
however, is not simply doing wrong, or committing some sin, or
violating some social canon; it is, rather, the necessary consequence of striving to be human. It lies at the juncture where
human will and human understanding engage the mysteries of the
universe. Odysseus' conscious choice to leave Calypso's island to
find again human life and human community apart from the
liminal and unreal existence with her means engaging a chaotic
world that, on the one hand, makes *cosmos* possible, but, on the
other, has within it the forces of his own destruction.

His choice, then, is a choice of vulnerability, weakness, and
limitation; that is to say, he finds meaning in his life by confronting the very possibility of losing it. Life only has meaning when
contemplated from the perspective of its opposite, from the
possibility, indeed the inevitability of death. To become a god is to
lose limitation, vulnerability, to lose those very things by which the
essence of being human is defined and realized. Odysseus' rejection of Calypso's offer of immortality is not some suicidal death
wish; it is rather an affirmation of his humanity, of his zest for life,
of his desire to live to the fullest measure of his mortality. Beye
writes of this choice:

> God, who is not only immortal, but also finally omni-
> present and invincible, can never know limitation of any

sort. He cannot therefore create life in the living of it, establish boundaries to a psyche, and define the way.
Eternity, ubiquity, and insensibility are not only hard to
grasp, they are stultifying in their implications. Odysseus' most profound manifestation of his essential heroism is a rejection of Calypso's offer.[47]

Another way of illustrating the point is to retell the Indone-
sian myth of the Stone and the Banana:

In the beginning, the sky was very near to the earth, and
the Creator used to let down his gifts to men at the end
of a rope. One day he thus lowered a stone. But the Ancestors would have none of it, and called out to their
Maker, 'What have we to do with this stone? Give us
something else.' God complied; some time later, he let
down a banana, which they joyfully accepted. Then the
ancestors heard a voice from heaven saying, 'Because ye
have chosen the banana, your life shall be like its life.
When the banana-tree has offspring, the parent stem
dies; so shall ye die and your children shall step into
your place. Had ye chosen the stone, your life would
have been like the life of the stone, changeless and immortal.'[48]

This story well illustrates the nature of Odysseus' choice.
While the stone, on the one hand, represents indestructibility and
invulnerability, it also symbolizes denseness, inertia, and immobil-
ity. Life, on the other hand, is marked by growth, change, development, and openness to new possibilities through creativity and
freedom.[49] Thus Odysseus' rejection of Calypso's offer is both a
rejection of immortality and the stone-like immutability inherent
in it, while at the same time a profound affirmation of life and its
potentialities. The rejection of immortality with its implicit
affirmation of humanity necessarily involves a confrontation with
the chaotic and the very real possibility of annihilation. The
measure of heroic humanity, then, is the strength and willingness
to run that risk. Odysseus' liminal movement from chaos to order,
which is the underlying pattern of the *Odyssey,* is a movement

from death to life. It is also a journey fraught with manifold dangers. For the possibility of annihilation is present in every endeavor to transcend human limitations. This is the reality that lies behind the paradoxical and ambiguous nature of Odysseus' *apotheosis*, couched as it is in the imagery of chaos and cosmos.

Notes to Chapter IV

[1] For examples and an interesting discussion of the epic *nostoi,* the reader is referred to George Huxley, "the Returns of the Heroes from Troy," in his *Greek Epic Poetry from Eumelos to Panyassis* (Cambridge: Harvard University Press, 1969), 162–173.

[2] I have borrowed Homer's word (*Od.* 1.1), which I understand to mean "of many turns" in the sense that it points to both the multiplicity of the hero's experiences as well as the multiplicity of symbolic meanings the hero comes to embody. Cf. Pietro Pucci, *Odysseus Polutropos: Intertextual Readings in the Odyssey and the Iliad* (Ithaca: Cornell University Press, 1987), 14.

[3] Charles Segal, "Transition and Ritual in Odysseus' Return" *La Parola Del Passato* 22 (1967), 321–342.

[4] *Ibid.,* 322.

[5] Bruce Louden, *The Odyssey, Structure, Narration and Meaning* (Baltimore: The Johns Hopkins University Press, 1999), 27–28

[6] Ibid., 28

[7] Ibid., 324.

[8] Cf. Louden's discussion, *ibid.,* 76–87.

[9] Louden, *ibid.,* 124.

[10] Ibid.

[11] Cf. *Il.* 21.240–1, 263, 268, 306, and *Od.* 5.296–332, 9.80. See also Louden's discussion of the phrase, *ibid.,* 124–129.

[12] Cf. the discussion of Achilles at the Scamander, above, 65.

[13] Louden, *ibid.,* 106.

[14] Cf. Dimock's discussion of this etymology, George E. Dimock Jr., "The Name of Odysseus," *The Hudson Review,* vol. IX, no. 1 (Spring 1956), 52–70. Reprinted in George Steiner and Robert Fagles, *Homer, A Collection of Critical Essays* (Englewood Cliffs, NJ: Prentice Hall, 1962), 106–121. This quote is from p. 111 of this collection.

[15] A kind of veil or wimple, perhaps similar to the mantilla worn by Spanish women. For a fascinating discussion of this word's semantic range in the Homeric poems, see Dianna Rhyan Kardulias, "Odysseus in Ino's Veil: Feminine Headdress and the Hero in *Odyssey* 5" *TAPA* 131 (2001), 23–51.

[16] B. Holtsmark, "Spiritual Rebirth of the Hero: *Odyssey* 5." *Classical Journal* 61 (February, 1966), 206–210.

[17] Dimock writes: "Leaving Calypso is very like leaving the perfect security and satisfaction of the womb," *ibid*. He is wrong, however, with his bald statement, "the womb is a deadly place." To be sure, it is a place of pre-existence, but pre-existence is something different than death. Rather, the womb is a place of liminality, which leads to birth and existence in human community. To be in the womb is to be betwixt and between, in the interstices of becoming and being.

[18] Cf. *L.S.J.* sub χάρις, II.2.

[19] Cf. for example, the flood stories in Sumerian, Babylonian, and Hebrew myth, and the discussion in the following chapter.

[20] Jonathan Shay, Achilles in Vietnam: Combat Trauma and the Undoing of Character (New York: Atheneum, 1994).

[21] Cf. Heubeck, West, and Hainsworth, *A Commentary on Homer's Odyssey, Volume I: Introduction and Books I–VIII* (Oxford: Clarendon Press, 1988), 15–16.

[22] Shay, *Achilles in Vietnam* (note 20 above), 10.

[23] This interpretation sees Phaeacia not so much as a fairy-tale land, but as the idealized, almost perfect society of Odysseus' recollection. The sophistication and culture of the Phaeacians—especially as represented by Nausicaa—contrast with the boorish cruelty of the suitors on Ithaca. It is worth noting, in particular, that Nausicaa's modesty, decorum and sense of propriety sharply contrast with the behavior of the serving girls in Odysseus' palace, who sleep with the suitors. This pointed contrast between the society of Phaeacia and the social chaos of Ithaca suggests the moral perspective Odysseus brings with him when he returns to Ithaca and exacts his punishment of the suitors and their paramours.

[24] Cf. Heubeck, West, and Hainsworth, *A Commentary* (note 21 above), 20.

25 Dimock, "The Name of Odysseus," 116.

26 The Roman poet Tibullus takes up these Phaeacian themes of dreams, unreality and recognition in I.3 of his *Elegies*. Cf. D. H. Mills, "Tibullus and Phaeacia, a Reinterpretation of I.3." *The Classical Journal*, Vol. 69 (1974), 226–233.

27 See Charles Beye, *The Iliad, Odyssey, and Epic Tradition* (London: Macmillan, 1968), 180–81.

28 Ibid., 109.

29 Dimock, "The Name of Odysseus" 109.

30 Cf. D. H. Mills, "Odysseus and Polyphemus: Two Homeric Similes Reconsidered," *The Classical Outlook*, 58 (May–June 1981), 97–99.

31 Steve Reece, The Stranger's Welcome: Oral Theory and the Aesthetics of the Homeric Hospitality Scene (Ann Arbor: University of Michigan Press, 1993), 130.

32 See Holtsmark, "Rebirth," (note 16 above) 207, who also refers to Whitman's observation of his "utter submersion of identity" (*Homer and the Heroic Tradition*, 298).

33 Αἴθυια. This bird is variously identified as the cormorant, shearwater, sea-crow, herring gull, coot, curlew, puffin, grebe, or diving tern. Cf. M. Detienne in his essay "The Sea Crow" (in R. L. Gordon, ed. *Myth, Religion and Society: Structuralist Essays*, New York: Cambridge University Press, 1981), 17.

34 Cf. Joseph Fontenrose, "White Goddess and Syrian Goddess," *University of California Publications in Semitic Philology*, Vol. 11, 125–148, and the same author's "The Sorrows of Ino and of Procne," *TAPA* 79 (1948), 125–167, and L. R. Farnell, "Ino-Leucothea," *JHS* XXXVI (1916), 36–44.

35 Cf. Walter Burkert, *Structure and History in Greek Mythology and Ritual* (Berkeley, University of California Press, 1979), 57–58.

36 Fontenrose, "White Goddess," (note 34 above) 147.

37 The Greek word for immortal is ἄμβροτος, which is etymologically related to ἀμβροσία, the divine food of the gods which nourishes them, and on another occasion is used to keep dead bodies from corruption (a

kind of divine formaldehyde). Thus this veil seems to take on some of the life-preserving qualities of ἀμβροσία. It is also significant in this connection that later Greeks understood Ino's veil to be the purple fillet which the initiates of the Samothracian mysteries wore to protect themselves from the dangers of the sea. Cf. Scholiast to Apollonius Rhodius, 1.917.

[38] One might also suggest that this mythic pattern of a maternal relation between immortal goddess and mortal son is a faint reflection of the relation between the primordial *Magna Mater* and her subordinate spouse/consort. Pucci, *Odysseus Polutropos* (note 2 above), 64, sees a sexual dimension in the encounter: "The titillating pleasure of sex surfaces in the form of a beautiful deity and her discreet gesture."

[39] M. Detienne in his essay "The Sea Crow" (in R. L. Gordon, ed. *Myth, Religion and Society*), argues that one can view Athena as *Athena of the Sea*, in the sense that there is in the *Odyssey* a whole series of interventions by this goddess in "the context of the sea and navigation" (16). He focuses on the theriomorphic identification of Athena with the αἴθυια, the 'sea-crow'. Thus when Ino-Leucothea, having provided for Odysseus' salvation, departs in the form of this bird, the parallelism of the two goddesses is established. This parallelism moreover, suggests the soteriological importance of Athena's stilling the storm after Odysseus' shipwreck, so that he might "escape death and the spirits of death" (θάνατον καὶ κῆρας, 5.387); she too, no less that Ino-Leucothea, is responsible for his salvation. Cf. also the discussion of Ino-Leucothea in Frederick Ahl and Hanna M. Roisman, *The Odyssey Re-formed* (Ithaca: Cornell University Press, 1996), 45–46.

[40] Homer uses a subtle word play to suggest the unique relation between Odysseus and Ino-Leucothea when he describes her as one who "obtained a share" (ἐξέμμορε) of divine honor (5.335), and then a few lines later (5.339), Odysseus himself as "ill-fated" (κάμμορος, literally, "having a share of woe").

[41] Shay, *Achilles in Vietnam* (note 20 above), 51.

[42] Ann Bergren sees Ino-Leucothea "allegorized" as midwife: "In an attempt to facilitate his separation from the sea, she urges him to take off the garments from Calypso that have covered him like a placenta, but now hold him back (342–345)." (Ann T. Bergren, "Allegorizing Winged Words: Simile and Symbolization in *Odyssey* V," *Classical World* 74 [October 1980], 119.)

43 Kardulias (*op. cit.* note 15 above, 34, 41) sees Ino's veil as a "powerful instrument of boundary magic" and a token of Odysseus' liminality. Having herself crossed the boundary between mortal and immortal, Ino now gives it to Odysseus to facilitate his passage from immortal to mortal life. She also argues that when Odysseus dons the veil, it is an act of transvestism, which frequently occurs in liminal contexts.

44 I would emphasize *hero* at this point to justify the appropriateness of the term apotheosis; for the epic hero, by any definition, is a notch above ordinary humanity, hence closer to the gods.

45 Cf. the *Cypria* as reported in Proclus' *Chrestomathy*, i, and Hyginus *Fabulae* 95.2.

46 Cf. George Dimock, *The Unity of the Odyssey* (Amherst, MA: The University of Massachusetts Press, 1989), 70.

47 Beye, *Epic Tradition*, (note 27 above) 189.

48 Quoted by Mircea Eliade, "Mythologies of Death: An Introduction" in Frank E. Reynolds and Earle H. Waugh, *Religious Encounters with Death: Insights from the History and Anthropology of Religion* (University Park, PA.: The Pennsylvania State U. Press, 1977), 16, quoting J. G. Frazer, *The Belief in Immortality*, vol. I (London, 1913), 74–75, quoting A. C. Kruit (=*From Primitives to Zen*, 140).

49 Eliade, *ibid.*

❈
Chapter V
Old Testament Patterns: Creation, Flood, Exodus

One of the most striking aspects of the use of mythic chaos in the Old Testament is the number of parallels between its flood story and other Near Eastern flood narratives. In fact, these similarities engendered much of the nineteenth century's intense interest in Babylonian studies, and the consequent growth of Near Eastern studies has continued unabated ever since.

In order to deal with the Old Testament flood story in the light of its Near Eastern affinities and bearing on mythic chaos, some preliminary observations are in order.

1) Floods occur in many geographic areas of the world and seem to have been quite common in Mesopotamia, as the archaeological record reveals.[1] It is likely, then, that the inhabitants of this region had considerable experience with floods, which naturally is expressed in mythic narratives.

2) Because pre-scientific peoples generally seek to explain natural phenomena through mythic tales and folklore, it follows that many flood myths are wholly or partially etiological in motive.

3) Because mythic stories of a universal flood are typically set in primeval time, i.e., the "once upon a time when our ancestors lived," they tend to be connected with creation myths. Myths about the world's origin, its destruction by a universal flood, and its subsequent re-creation and repopulation are often interrelated in the imagination of prescientific peoples.[2] Implicit in these myths is the notion of chaos: the flood is seen as a return of the chaos existing before creation; similarly, the end of the flood and the retreat of its waters is a new beginning, a re-creation of the cosmos.

4) Although often etiological in motive and purpose, stories of creation and flood are not told simply to satisfy historical or

scientific curiosity; rather they have a vital communal function. By means of recitation—a ritual act in its own right—or dramatic presentation, flood stories address critical moments in the life of the community. The power of myth is such that, in the minds of the mythographers and their audiences, the meaning of human existence is deeply rooted in the myth that tells of man's first appearance on the earth; the retelling of the myth has the power to ensure the continuity of human life. Similarly, retelling the myth of the great flood and the world's subsequent repopulation is a ritual *re-creation* that guarantees the continuation of the species.[3]

5) Since explanations of the great flood are often predicated upon the existence of divine powers conceived in anthropomorphic terms, floods are seen as a result of the gods' anger. This conception is in the nature of an analogy: as human beings become angry and engage in destructive behavior, so also the personified powers of nature manifest destructive anger. Because human misbehavior is frequently the occasion of divine anger, flood stories often have a moral dimension.[4] Moreover, the presence of an ethical element often expresses social crisis: something is amiss in the human community and needs divine intervention and correction. On occasion, the moral dimension is absent; the annihilating flood is merely evidence that the divinity who decided to create humankind can just as easily make the arbitrary decision to destroy it. As Westermann observes, the creation of humankind implies the possibility of its negation.[5] Hence, the social crisis implicit in flood myths reflects a profound anxiety: flood myths suggest the possibility of universal destruction, the death of the individual no less than the annihilation of the cosmos itself. This awareness of possible annihilation, seemingly peculiar to the human species, is the primordial fear, if I may so term it, that lies behind the vast multitude of flood myths.

But also present in the very nature of flood stories is the possibility of salvation. The divinities who have decided to eradicate humankind have a change of heart, and bring about its salvation through the preservation of one or more specially chosen individuals. Westermann writes of this possibility:

> And so a completely new dimension enters human existence: the continuation of existence because of a saving action. Salvation by an act of God, so important a religious phenomenon, is grounded in the primeval event of the flood story.[6]

6) After the flood, there is typically some kind of restoration, a resolution of the moral issues, an amelioration of the social crisis, or a return to pre-flood conditions. Significantly, the human response to the restoration becomes the pattern for subsequent repetition of ritual activities. Often there is a new agreement or covenant between humans and divine beings that seeks to prevent future floods or to provide recompense for the one just past. Not only is the crisis resolved, there is also an attempt to prevent its recurrence.

Mythic flood narratives, therefore, insofar as they seek to recreate a ritual pattern and call into play the powers inherent in that pattern, attempt to address the liminal concerns of their audience and the community of which it is a part. These narratives can be read as a *stabilizing strategy*[7] for addressing and ameliorating those conditions that threaten the community's well-being. For this reason such myths often contain stories of deliverance and salvation. They tell how a heroic individual and often the community to which he is connected avoided danger, death, or annihilation.

The Genesis Flood Narrative

The myth of the primeval waters of chaos yielding to cosmic order lies deeply embedded in the Old Testament creation narrative. In order to come to grips with this mythic pattern, it will be useful to make a few remarks about the first chapter of Genesis, and then to examine the story of Jacob at the ford of the Jabbok River, which has fascinating connections with the mythic pattern of watery chaos.

Since the time of Hermann Günkel,[8] it has been a commonplace of Old Testament scholarship that four major literary traditions have come together in the evolution of the Hebrew Bible. Two are important for the Genesis narratives of creation and the flood story, and both use mythic conceptions of wide currency in the Near East. The earlier of these two traditions is identified as the *Yahwist*, or J writer. This tradition traced the story of humankind from the creation of the world to a point just before the entrance of the Israelites into Canaan. Scholarly consensus places the composition of J ca. 960–930 BCE.[9]

The *Priestly Writer,* or P, worked in the late exilic or early restoration period, ca. 550–450 BCE. This writer was concerned to set forth the religious and ritual practices that distinguished Israel from other peoples (hence the denominative *Priestly Writer*). He is responsible, for example, for the detail of a seven-day creation story with God resting on the seventh, thus establishing the important parallel to the ritual features of the Sabbath observances.[10] The worldview of the *Priestly Writer* consists of a sophisticated mythic and cultic mixture, in which the movement from the ordered and orderly to the disordered and chaotic is at once fraught with chance and unpredictability, while at the same time subject to human control. Even in the midst of the impending chaos of the flood, Noah sets in order the pairs of animals entering the ark "two by two, male and female." Even in a setting of ritual and mythic liminality with all of its unknowns and facets of terror, we can recognize the cultic scrupulosity of the *Priestly Writer*. In that scrupulosity dwells the old primitive fear that is central to ritual liminality, the possible annihilation of all that is real and meaningful in the movement from the familiar and known to the strange and dangerous world of the chaotic and disordered.

The *Yahwist*, by contrast, seems more interested in the wider ramifications of his story, i.e. the mythic and theological meanings of his narrative. In particular, he sees a pattern of moral decline as he traces out the step-by-step increase in human sinfulness, beginning with the disobedience of Adam and Eve in the Garden of Eden, the story of Cain and Abel, and culminating with the Flood and the building of the Tower of Babel. In these narratives, Yahweh becomes increasingly frustrated and angry at human waywardness. When, therefore, the *Yahwist*, who clearly knows the Mesopotamian traditions, turns to the story of the Flood, he underscores the moral dimension of the story. God is angry and determines to limit, if not punish, human sinfulness.

Although the creation and flood narratives in Genesis with their monotheistic presuppositions have a theological intent very different from other Near Eastern myths, yet the mythic substratum is still partially visible. In particular, Gen 1.1–2 suggests watery chaos as the condition before creation, as "the spirit of God moves over the face of the deep." Not only does the word *face* recall the personifications of water in Greek and Babylonian mythology, the Hebrew word for *deep* (*tehom*) appears as though "it were a distant echo of the mythical battle with Tiamat, the female personification of the powers of chaos."[11] So also, the movement of God's spirit across the face of the deep may reflect Marduk's use of the winds in his battle with the chaotic powers of Tiamat.[12] In a similar way, Marduk's division of Tiamat's body into two parts, with the upper becoming the heavens, and the lower part the waters below the earth, may lie behind the Genesis conception of God separating the waters below from the waters above by the interposition of the firmament (Gen 1.3–8). The underlying mythic conception, then, is that of an orderly realm created between the two halves of a separated primal chaos. This notion recurs in the Flood Story when the *Priestly Writer* has the flood waters come from both the windows of heaven as well as the "fountains of the great deep" (Gen 7.11). Thus, the Genesis Flood Story envisions a return to the watery chaos antedating creation.

The notion of struggle, which is a consistent part of this mythic pattern, occurs only in the strange and problematic prologue to the Flood narrative (Gen 6.1–4):

> *When men began to multiply on the face of the ground, and daughters were born to them, the sons of God saw that the daughters of men were fair; and they took to wife such of them as they chose. Then the Lord said, 'My spirit shall not abide in man forever, for his is flesh, but his days shall be a hundred and twenty years.' The Nephilim were on the earth in those days, and also afterward, when the sons of God came in to the daughters of men, and they bore children to them. These were the mighty men that were of old, the men of renown.*

Despite the considerable controversy concerning these verses, a few comments can be made. While it is likely that the Nephilim had an origin apart from the flood narrative itself, nevertheless they are used to introduce the Flood Story. The underlying myth of the prologue seems to go back into the pre-monotheistic period of the Israelites as it explains the presence of the ancient heroes, the Nephilim,[13] who were the result of miscegenation between gods and human women. It seems clear, then, that reference to the Nephilim is intended to introduce the story of the Flood by suggesting, however obliquely, the reasons for divine anger and the resulting flood. Secondly, the narrator understands a conflict between God and humanity, the cause of which is the implicit challenge to God's sovereignty either by humans (who consequently suffer the shortening of their life span) or by the Nephilim and their intermarriage with human women. In any case, God reacts to the challenge to his sovereignty by reiterating the fact of human mortality: "My spirit shall not abide in man forever."[14] The word for "spirit" *(ruah)* means "the life breath of God by which man has become and remains a living being."[15] Because human life had its origin with him, God reasserts his authority to determine its end. In this way not only does the flood narrative provide an etiology for the length of human life, it also touches upon the connection between morality and mortality—a recurring element in this mythic pattern.

On this point Bruce Vawter makes a provocative suggestion about the meaning of the prologue in relation to early Israelite and Canaanite backgrounds. Noting that "man aspires to the divine," he goes on to argue that such an aspiration, far from being an act of *hubris*, "can be a legitimate desire for communion with God." One route, however, very common in Canaan and Babylonia, was ritual marriage or sacred prostitution, by which the temple prostitute or hierodule served as surrogate for the deity. (In a not dissimilar way, the humanization of Enkidu in the *Gilgamesh Epic* by the ministrations of a prostitute raises him from the animal to the human realm.) If Vawter is right in seeing the *hieros gamos* behind the myth of divine and human miscegenation,[16] then the target of the narrative's implicit censure is sacralized sexuality, the notion that sexuality somehow has the power to confer immortality. This Genesis narrative firmly rejects this notion, first by an oblique allusion to the ancient myth of the Nephilim, then by God's limiting human life span to 120 years, and finally by the drastic punishment of the great flood. God's sovereignty remains unchallenged.

Viewed in this way, the Genesis prologue to the story of the flood bears subtle affinities to Calypso's offer of marriage and immortality to Odysseus, and to Enkidu's humanization by a prostitute in the *Gilgamesh Epic*. Likewise, Gilgamesh's encounter with Siduri, the maker of ale, also points in the same direction.

Not only does she provide Gilgamesh with directions for his journey to Utnapishtim (where he hopes to find the secret of immortality), she also offers him a hedonistic philosophy as an anodyne for his obsession with mortality:

> *Thou, Gilgamesh, let full be thy belly, / Make thou merry by day and by night. / Of each day make thou a feast of rejoicing, / Day and night dance thou and play! / Let thy garments be sparkling fresh, / Thy head be washed; bathe thou in water. / Pay heed to the little one that holds on to thy hand, / Let thy spouse delight in thy bosom! / For this is the task of mankind!*[17]

Like Calypso in the *Odyssey*, Siduri is the mythic representation of hedonism as the answer to death.

We have seen that the mythologem of struggle with watery chaos in these epic encounters expresses the inner crisis of the heroic individual in terms both of hedonism and mortality. As in the *Odyssey* and the *Gilgamesh Epic*, the Genesis narrative portrays a cosmic and social crisis as a moral crisis leading to a redefinition of human mortality. Like the *Odyssey* and the *Gilgamesh Epic*, the Genesis narrative portrays a cosmic and social crisis through individuals, (making clear at the same time the relation between morality and mortality). To express it analogically: chaos is to the cosmos what death is to the individual. Our mythologem, then, portrays death as an aspect of chaos that threatens to undo human life and human endeavor. Moreover, the narratives of our concern suggest that sexuality may counter in some way the inevitability of death. But they all come to the conclusion that such a response is inadequate. Hedonism does not provide an antidote for mortality.

Noah's Liminality

The implicit contrast, therefore, between the immorality of the ancient Nephilim and the righteousness of Noah suggests the nature of his liminality. Noah's liminal separation is in reality his separation from the whole of humankind. That he is also the one who ultimately brings salvation is anticipated by the words of his father Lamech at his birth, "Out of the ground which the Lord has cursed this one shall bring us relief from our work and from the toil of our hands" (Gen. 5.29). Although the exact nature of the salvation Lamech envisions by these words is unclear, Noah's unique salvific status is patent. Likewise, his morality is repeatedly underscored: "But Noah found favor in the eyes of the Lord." (Gen. 6.8 *et passim*)

Like other liminal heroes, Noah struggles with chaos in the waters of the flood. Both the *Yahwist* and the *Priestly Writer*, moreover, make the connection between the moral chaos of the world and the flood itself. While the *Yahwist* identifies the moral chaos in the human spirit, "The Lord saw that the wickedness of [humankind] was great in the earth, and that every imagination of the thoughts of his heart was only evil continually" (Gen. 6.5), the *Priestly Writer* sees the moral chaos inherent in the world itself, "Now the earth was corrupt in God's sight, and the earth was filled with violence" (Gen. 6.11). One should note, therefore, that in the eyes of both writers primordial chaos returns in the moral corruption of the human race and the whole creation itself, no less than in the waters of the flood. Norman Habel notes:

> The situation which God must rectify in Genesis 6.9-11 however, is not primarily the evil of man as such, but the universal corruption at large in the earth. The earth is said to be 'corrupt' (*shahat*) and filled with 'violence' (*hamas*). Both of these Hebrew expressions suggest a chaotic force of destruction at work in the order of creation. The perspective seems to be cosmic.[18]

Hence, Noah's liminal struggle is both moral and cosmic because the post-flood world will be marked by a new cosmic and moral order, established by God's covenant on the one hand, and symbolized by the heavenly rainbow on the other. Noah's heroic status, therefore, derives from the fact that the very existence of the post-flood order rests solely with him.

Noah's period of liminal separation and testing encompasses the building of the ark as well as the flood itself, which lasts one year. It should be noted that the disorder and deadly chaos ordinarily associated with liminal separation is not specifically connected with Noah, but with the violence and destruction that both the *Yahwist* and *Priestly Writer* describe occurring outside of the ark. Indeed, within the ark all is order, regularity, and organization. The repeated phrase, "according to their kind" and the image of all the living creatures entering "two by two, male and female" suggest a microcosm of order within the ark over and against the watery chaos soon to come without.

Unlike Utnapishtim in the *Gilgamesh Epic* and other liminal heroes, Noah does not speak of his terrors during the flood. (In point of fact, Noah speaks no words at all during the whole of the flood narrative.[19] His simple obedience to God's commands seems intended to underscore his unique morality as God's chosen instrument for the world's salvation.) Nevertheless, the careful description of the broad devastation without, and God's words at the end of the flood promising that such a catastrophe will never happen again, suggest the implicit terror not only of Noah himself but also the entire human community in the face of such cosmic destruction.

God's Covenant and Liminal Reintegration

Noah's reintegration comes with his exit from the ark. The important elements are not only the ritual reincorporation suggested by Noah's burnt offerings to the Lord but also the promise of renewal and salvation made explicit by the covenant and God's promise never again to destroy the earth by flood.

In the mythology of liminal passage, social crisis is often conceived in terms of cosmic crisis. In making this identification, the

Genesis narrative expresses a conception of the world in which God defeated chaos at the time of creation, and confronts it a second time with Noah and the ark. Myth and ritual come together in Noah's ritual sacrifice of clean animals and burnt offering (Gen. 8.20), and God's response never again to curse the ground because of human sinfulness (Gen. 8.21). The consequence of this second defeat of chaos is a new cosmic order marked by an everlasting pattern of seasonal and diurnal order: "While the earth remains, seedtime and harvest, cold and heat, summer and winter, day and night, shall not cease." (Gen. 8.22) Noah's role is clear; his ritual sacrifice insures that the floodwaters of chaos will never recur. (Although the *Yahwist* uses a somewhat primitive theological concept—God smells the pleasant odor of the sacrifice and promises no more floods—the cause and effect relation between Noah's act and God's response is clear.)

In this way, the focus of the flood narrative begins with a social crisis occasioned by the actions of the Nephilim and moves from the societal perspective to the unique liminal individual, Noah. It is through the liminality of this individual that ultimately human society is redeemed. There is, then, the profound irony that the social order is preserved through its own destruction and through the one liminal individual who, although remote and isolated from the human community, survives to reconstitute not only a new social order but also a new relationship between humankind and God.

Jacob at the Jabbok

Genesis tells also of a heroic battle with a water deity in the story of Jacob's struggle at the Jabbok River (Gen 32.22). There are indications that Jacob's antagonist had originally been a river spirit, whose defeat was necessary for his crossing of the river.[20] Like Gilgamesh, Achilles, and Odysseus, Jacob becomes a liminal figure, separated from his community as he flees his brother Esau and wanders in an alien land. The cause of his exile is the theft of his father's blessing, which, like the earlier theft of his brother's birthright, involves questions of identity, honor, and social status.[21] His eventual reconciliation with Esau marks the end of his liminality and the beginning of his reintegration, which leads to a new understanding of his place in the world and of his relation to his descendants. Michael Fishbane has called the story *Jacob Agonistes*, "for it contains his many struggles to establish himself in the world."[22]

This story is important to this study because it has clear thematic and symbolic affinities with the mythologem of heroic encounter with the chaotic as its liminal hero struggles with a watery power able to destroy him. The river is the boundary of the liminal, and, given the importance of the liminal as an expression of the chaotic in all the heroic struggles thus far considered, crossing the river is for Jacob the *sine qua non* of his heroic liminality and heroic struggle. In considering Jacob's story, I wish to focus on three important details: the conferring of the blessing and its relation to the naming of Jacob/Israel; the meaning of the *face to face* encounter with Esau; and, finally, the motif of mortality/immortality.

The Genesis account has eschewed description of the Jabbok river itself: Frazer, however, has supplied a geographic description that echoes Homer's wild Scamander:

> The gorge is, in the highest degree, wild and picturesque. On either hand the cliffs rise almost perpendicularly to a great height; you look up the precipices or steep declivities to the skyline far above. At the bottom of this mighty chasm the Jabbok flows with a powerful current, its blue-gray water fringed and hidden, even at a short distance, by a dense jungle of tall oleanders, whose crimson blossoms add a glow of colour to the glen in early summer. The Blue River, for such is its modern

name, runs fast and strong. Even in ordinary times the water reaches to the horses' girths, and sometimes the stream is quite unfordable, the flood washing grass and bushes high up the banks on either hand.[23]

One is naturally led to ask why Jacob would undertake the dangerous crossing of such a river in the dark of night. Two answers may be suggested: first, the night-time crossing is designed to balance the vision at Bethel, when, on his outward journey, Jacob "stopped there that night, because the sun had set"; as he slept that night, he experienced the vision of the ladder reaching to heaven, and heard God's promise of numerous descendants and possession of the very land on which he slept. Upon waking, Jacob called the name of the place Bethel, "the House of God" (Gen 28.11). Thus, the two nocturnal hierophanies frame Jacob's period of liminality[24] and mark the boundaries within which he discovers his identity and place in the world. Jacob's liminal alienation is preparation for his destined greatness.

The second point is that Jacob's nocturnal struggle with God prefigures his morning encounter with Esau. This is Fishbane's interpretation: during the night, Jacob sees "God face to face" (Gen. 32.33). On the next day, when he has been reconciled with Esau, he says: "for truly to see your face is like seeing the face of God" (33.10). On this reading, Jacob is working through his anticipated encounter with Esau by a kind of dream in which the blessings of God insuring his superiority to his elder brother become the very figure with whom he wrestles. Insofar as his meeting with his brother is symbolic of social reintegration, the wrestling with God is the liminal struggle that prepares for his return and reintegration. His victory, moreover, becomes a restatement of the blessing. Fishbane again:

In the 'night encounter' Jacob wrestles with the
'Esau' he carried within him. The 'rebirth' Jacob
achieves by his psychic victory in the night had still
to be confirmed in the light of day. Jacob awakens
with the deep conviction that he had faced his
struggle with courage and had been blessed by divinity. He greets the morning light with the glow of
his own self-transformation and illumination. Having seen Elohim face to face at Penuel, Jacob can
prepare to meet Esau face to face as well.[25]

As a mythic expression of ritual reincorporation, the story of
the Jabbok also has to do with Jacob's heroic identity and his new
understanding of it; both the change of his name to Israel and the
blessing pronounced by the nocturnal antagonist suggest his new,
post-liminal, place in society.

The two events are related. In the first, Jacob is told, "Your
name shall no more be called Jacob, but Israel" (v. 28). In the
second, Jacob asks his adversary's name, but instead of an answer,
he receives a blessing. To assess the meaning of this strange
interchange, it is useful to recall the primitive belief that knowledge of a person's name confers power over him, as the previous
discussion of Odysseus and the Cyclops has shown. The story's
two antagonists are not equal; one knows his adversary's name,
the other does not. The issue is power, and even though Jacob is
blessed, power is in the hands of his adversary. If we understand
that the issue of power here involves sovereignty and control, it
becomes clear that Jacob's struggle with God in the guise of the
river deity not only contains the implicit mythic notion of struggle
with chaos, it also addresses the social crisis by establishing the
respective sovereignty of God and Jacob. God's sovereignty is
symbolized by his knowledge of and his changing Jacob's name;
Jacob's sovereignty results from the divine blessing and the
promise of greatness for his descendants. From this struggle,
then, a new order is created in which both adversaries have been

victorious. Jacob/Israel will become the nation's venerated patriarch, but with the clear understanding that his human sovereignty is inextricably connected to God's cosmic sovereignty.[26]

Also involved in this story is the issue of mortality. As Jacob crosses the boundary, he comes face to face with an ambiguous power (it is initially unclear whether his antagonist is human or divine) that can either destroy or save him. Jacob concludes: "I have seen God face to face, and yet my life has been preserved" (Gen. 32.30). As has been seen in the other narratives of watery conflict, the hero engages a life and death struggle. His success raises him beyond the usual limits of human life: Odysseus is reborn from the sea; Achilles is transformed into a raging conflagration consuming everything in his path; Gilgamesh completes the all but impossible trek to Utnapishtim to learn the truth of human mortality and his own inevitable death; Noah receives God's covenant; and here Jacob sees God face to face, lives to tell of it, and goes on to achieve the status of eponymous progenitor of the Israelite nation.

Chaos and Creation

Up to this point, watery chaos has typically been a destructive power that must be defeated. The Old Testament authors, however, also see in the powers of the watery realm an instrument of creation, that is, a beneficial tool in the hands of God for furthering his creative and salvific purposes. Jacob's encounter at the Jabbok, with its promise of a new people, is part of a larger pattern of creation. It is the first stage of God's creative relationship with the people of Israel. At a later point he *creates* the nation of Israel by leading his chosen people out of Egypt and drowning their enemies in the flood of the sea. The clearest evidence for this movement from destructive to creative chaos occurs in the Song of the Sea (Exodus 15.1-18), in which Moses and the Israelites sing of their deliverance from the Egyptians. The song uses the imagery of battle against the forces of watery chaos:

> *At the blast of thy nostrils the waters piled up, / the floods stood up in a heap; / the deeps congealed in the heart of the sea. / Thou didst blow with thy wind, the sea covered them* (15.8, 10).[27]

God wages battle against the Egyptians, who are conceived as enemies of both God and the Israelites. The watery powers of chaos are now an instrument of God's will. This transformation of chaos into a vehicle of redemption reflects the different emphases in the creation stories of the *Priestly Writer* and the *Yahwist*. Where the *Priestly Writer* of Genesis simply has the flood symbolize watery chaos, with the *Yahwist*, the waters of the deep become the waters of irrigation by which God brings about the growth of vegetation, and by which (implicitly at least) he creates man from the dust of the earth:

> *but a mist [flood] went up from the earth and watered the whole face of the ground—then the Lord God formed man of dust from the ground* (Gen. 2.6–7).

Thus, watery chaos becomes the source of plant and animal growth, the beginning of humankind; in short, chaos is the matrix of human life.[28]

The imagery of flood and a cosmic battle with the forces of the sea in destruction of the Egyptians also involves a moral parallel. As God punished human wickedness at the time of the Flood, so also the Egyptians are rightly punished for their immoral treatment of the Israelites. The imagery of the Exodus passage suggests that the nature of Egyptian wickedness is akin to that of greed and gluttony: "The enemy said: 'I will divide the spoil, my desire shall have its fill of them'" (15.9). The imagery of arrogant gluttony on the part of the Egyptians parallels the hubristic expectation of immortality in the prologue to the Flood narrative.

The Song of the Sea in Exodus, then, brings together three dimensions implicit in the mythologem of watery chaos:

1) The cosmic battle between the creator deity and the chaotic powers of the sea.

2) The creative and salvific powers of the chaotic waters in the Yahwist vision of God creating plant and human life through the beneficent irrigating waters of the land.

3) The issue of human morality reflected in the punishment of Egyptian arrogance and wickedness.

The Ritualization of Myth

Not only does the mythologem of heroic battle with watery chaos figure in the epics of the Greek and Mesopotamian peoples, it also receives ritual expression. The Akitu festival of the Babylonians is one example. The story of Marduk's victory over Tiamat was incorporated into the Babylonian New Year Festival and was solemnly recited in the temple of Marduk on the fourth day of the *Akitu*. In a celebration of his victory over the forces of chaos in the person of Tiamat, the Babylonians formally paraded the god's image through their city, and concluded the ritual with its installation in a special shrine.

As part of the ritual, the reigning king was formally deposed and then reinstated. Thus, the festival commemorated the renewal of life symbolically paralleling the original creation of the cosmos; similarly, the re-enthronement of the king parallels the mythic re-establishment of cosmic order (after the flood?), and reconfirms his religious and political authority. In this way, the myth and the festival come together to express the connection between cosmic and political order. Just as Marduk overcame the powers of chaos and created cosmic order, so also the king's authority to establish and uphold order in the political community is publicly and religiously reaffirmed.[29] Not only does the myth explain the world and its order through ritual, it also legitimizes political structure.

Through ritual, the community also gives expression to a religious sensibility, which is a part of its self-understanding; at the same time, its political order is raised to cosmic significance. To put it another way, the primitive fear that the world and its sustaining order might one day relapse into primordial chaos is countered by the ritual reenactment of creation and the ritual re-enthronement of the king. The social crisis, occasioned by the coming of the new year (perhaps marked by the winter solstice), compels ritual action. Not only does the annual ritual put the celebrants into contact with the eternal verities of the cosmos and its recurring rhythms, it also provides the opportunity to act in such a way as to insure and maintain the continuation of the cosmic pattern, the very order of both universe and community.

Mettinger sees a similar phenomenon at work in the Hebrew Autumn Festival.[30] Arguing that the Autumn Festival of the early Israelites had mythological affinities with Canaanite thought, and "presumably was also related to the Mesopotamian Akitu Festival" (69), he concludes that it was conceptualized in the form of God's battle with the powers of Chaos. Citing Old Testament passages such as Ps. 74.12–17, 89.6–19 and 29.10 ("The Lord sits enthroned over the flood; the Lord sits enthroned as king for ever."), he suggests:

> The pre-exilic Autumn Festival, which lasted one week (Deut 16.13, 15), probably from the first to the seventh of Tishri, was a celebration characterized by the notions of the kingship of God, his victory over Chaos, and the subsequent Creation of the world.[31]

Insofar as it was a harvest festival, celebrating the fruitfulness of the earth as a blessing from God, the Autumn Festival had conceptual and typological connections with both the priestly and

Yahwist versions of creation. Moreover, as Mettinger argues, it developed in such a way that the Passover festival ultimately replaced it.[32] The Autumn Festival, then, looked back equally to the Flood and the Exodus events (both being times of social crisis). Expressing itself mythically through the idea of watery chaos, it also incorporated mythic conceptions of chaos into the ritual life of the early Israelites.

The Historicization of Myth

Mythological conceptions and their innate patterns of meaning often yield to new understandings and perceptions, sometimes even undergoing a radical shift in cognitive orientation. Specifically in the case of Old Testament writers, the mythic pattern of battle with watery chaos became a formative element in the development of historical consciousness among the Old Testament Israelites. Their conceptions of themselves as a people, that is to say, their national identity, and their understanding of their relation to God were influenced by the mythic ideas of chaos, conflict, and creation.

To illustrate: the Genesis flood narrative represents God releasing the chaotic forces of the sea to destroy man and his wickedness; but he also brings the flood to an end, restoring order, and, following a frequent Old Testament theme, he makes a covenant with man through Noah.[33] It is clear that these events relate typologically to the mythic battle with the sea, which lies behind the Genesis creation narratives. The flood, then, not only looks back to creation, it also becomes paradigmatic for the Exodus, the event in which God's destruction of the Egyptians in the flood of the sea is instrumental in the creation of the Israelite nation. In this way, the mythic pattern of heroic conquest of the watery chaos is historicized into the nation's traditions of self-identity. In describing this "historicizing tendency," Mettinger uses the expression "from myth to salvation history."[34] This

means that the mythic pattern not only becomes part of a historical consciousness, it also contributes to the development of the
Old Testament's unique theological perspectives.

In order to understand what it is about the mythologem that
lends itself to this development, it will be useful to reexamine its
basic structure and movement. Specifically, what is the relationship between the mythic pattern itself and the concepts of historical time to which it seems to have an innate affinity?

By way of answer to this question, it can be argued that the
myth of primordial conflict with watery chaos was subsumed by
Israelite experience and mentality into a broader, more universal
or archetypal pattern, to wit, a pattern of movement from order to
chaos and back again to order. Fishbane, for example, notes that
the Genesis account sees in the flood an event that "reverses the
created order and reestablishes primeval chaos." "Just so," he
goes on to argue, "the limitation of chaos which follows is an
explicit act or recreation."35 As has been suggested, this pattern
also shapes the Exodus experience in and through both the Autumn and the Passover festivals. The meaning of the pattern,
however, has radically changed by being appropriated and adapted
to the Exodus event. Previously used as a normative pattern for
the ritual (and therefore repetitive) Akitu and Autumn festivals, it
was simply an annual rite, in which the cyclical alternation of
chaos and order was understood to continue *in perpetuum*. The
appropriation of the pattern to the Exodus event, however, fundamentally altered the nature of the mythic paradigm; it became
finite, and in so doing, it became essentially historical. To put it
another way, the mythic notion of cyclical history—and seasonal
rituals reinforce the notion of history's cyclical movement—
corresponds nicely with the conceptual underpinnings of the
cosmic battle mythologem, especially when used in the rituals of
annual festivals. But when the mythologem is applied to the
Exodus event, it moves into the realm of history. The mythic and

cyclical pattern undergoes a permutation into a consciousness of history as linear motion through time. This means that even though the Exodus event was consistently expressed by Israelite writers and poets as God's cosmic battle with and through the powers of watery chaos, it was, nevertheless, crucial to their "invention" of history and the growth of their historical consciousness.

One aspect of this changed perspective is that the typical terror of the initiand during his ritual liminality becomes part of the historical experiences of a people. The Babylonian exile and its associated terrors, no less that the similar apprehensions at the time of the exodus from Egypt, can be termed a historical liminality, and the separation of a nation from the familiar and known is no less terrifying. Consequently, both the *Priestly Writer* and the *Yahwist* were intuitively sensitive to the mythic and cultic pattern of liminality and imbued their narratives with the affective qualities associated with the ritual liminality of ancient peoples generally.

The importance of this fundamental change in the conceptualization and employment of the mythic pattern cannot be overstated. Whereas other ancient religions and mythologies depended on the cycles of the season, or other recurrent phenomena (e.g., the annual flooding of the Nile), to give meaning to their lives and to put them into contact with the eternally recurring patterns and rhythms of the universe, ancient Israel parted company with such ideas. Not in the mythic, but in the realm of history is ultimate meaning to be found.[36]   Having rejected the prevailing cultic understanding of creation in terms of a dramatic or ritual reenactment of the primordial cosmic conflict, the Israelites centered their faith on the conviction of *historical* redemption.[37]   The significant event for them is no longer the creation of the world in the mythic *Urzeit*, but rather God's unique and decisive act in creating their nation in historical time.[38]

Conclusion

The presence of the mythic heroic battle with watery chaos in several pieces of ancient literatures has profoundly affected both their form and the content. Of the mythologem's various permutations perhaps the most interesting and conceptually provocative occurs in the Old Testament. Although it opens out to encompass larger and more comprehensive patterns of meaning, yet it retains its focus on the unique, heroic individual. The separation of Jacob from his brother Esau, for example, is part of a pattern that underlies many Biblical narratives. All the same, the mythologem of heroic battle with chaos becomes altered to express the social crisis of a people experiencing the dislocation of national exile and enslavement. Exile is chaos. The exile of Israel twists with terror. It is life cut off from God's presence. It is the reversal of the Exodus and the conquest. Indeed, it is a return to Ur of Babylon, or to the time of Noah with its return to primordial watery chaos. The exile of man from paradise, or man from God, is here crystallized as a crisis of national proportions.[39]

The terror of Odysseus before Poseidon's sea, the terror of Achilles before the raging Scamander, the terror of Gilgamesh at the prospect of his own death, and the terror of Jacob facing his unknown antagonist at the Jabbok become in the hand of the Old Testament historians and prophets a nation's fear for its survival and its hope for redemption. Perceiving the significance of the mythic pattern in this way, we can appreciate how profoundly mythopoetic are the literatures of the Babylonians, the Greeks, and especially the Old Testament historical writers, both in thought patterns and in the underlying archetypal structures. Moreover, in the hands of the Old Testament writers, the mythopoesis moves even further, becoming the basis of Israel's historical consciousness.

Notes to Chapter V

[1] Cf. Lambert, W. G., and A. R. Millard *Atrahasis, The Babylonian Story of the Flood*, with the Sumerian Flood Story by M. Civil (London: Oxford U. Press, 1969), 16. Cf. also Stephanie Dalley, *Myths from Mesopotamia: Creation, The Flood, Gilgamesh and Others* (Oxford: Oxford University Press, 1989), 4.

[2] In the *Atrahasis Epic* as in *Genesis*, the flood narrative follows closely upon the story of man's creation.

[3] Claus Westermann, *Genesis 1–11: A Commentary*, translated by John J. Scullion (Minneapolis: Augsburg Publishing House, 1984), 200.

[4] In at least two stories the cause of divine anger is human overpopulation; the Greek epic *Cypria* has Zeus contrive war to deal with the problem of excessive human population, and the Babylonian *Atrahasis* attributes the great flood to the gods' desire to set limits on burgeoning human populations. In the Hebrew version the spilling of human blood, and in Ovid's *Metamorphoses,* man's wickedness causes divine anger and punishment through a universal flood.

[5] Westermann, *op. cit.* (note 3 above), 52.

[6] Westermann, *ibid.*

[7] I am indebted to Gottwald, *The Hebrew Bible: A Socio-Literary Introduction* (Philadelphia: Fortress Press, 1985), 473, for this useful term.

[8] Hermann Günkel, *Schöpfung und Chaos in Urzeit und Endzeit* (Göttingen: Vandenhoeck und Ruprecht, 1895). In fact, the aim of Günkel's book is to describe a particular worldview based on the notion of the struggle between order and chaos.

[9] Gottwald, *ibid.,* 137.

[10] Gottwald, *ibid.* 140.

[11] B. W. Anderson, *Creation Versus Chaos: The Reinterpretation of Mythical Symbolism in the Bible* (New York: Association Press, 1967), 39. Anderson also notes the scholarly consensus "that there is a linguistic relation between the Hebrew *Tehom* and Babylonian Tiamat." See also Susan Niditch, *Chaos to Cosmos: Studies in Biblical Patterns of Creation* (Chico, CA: Scholars Press, 1985), 18.

[12] Anderson, *Creation, ibid*, 39.

[13] The word seems to mean the "mighty" or "strong ones," and is translated in the Septuagint by the Greek word γίγαντες. See Gerhard Von Rad, *Genesis, A Commentary* (Philadelphia: Westminster Press, 1961), 115.

[14] Gen. 6.3. All Old Testament translations are from the RSV.

[15] Bruce Vawter, *On Genesis: A New Reading* (Garden City, NY: Doubleday, 1977), 111.

[16] Vawter, *ibid*, 112–13.

[17] *ANET* 90

[18] Norman C. Habel, "The Two Flood Stories in Genesis" in his *Literary Criticism of the Old Testament* (Philadelphia: Fortress Press, 1971), 16.

[19] The only words we ever hear from Noah are the curse of slavery he utters against Canaan, the descendant of Ham, who saw and covered his drunken father's nakedness (Gen. 9.20–27). This problematic story, which seems to be using the awareness of nakedness as symbolic of sin, should probably be read as looking backward to the cause of expulsion from Eden and forward to the taking of Canaan, the Promised Land.

[20] A. B. Lord, *The Singer of Tales* (Cambridge: Harvard University, 1964), 197 n.2, and the references at 197 n.26.

[21] This theft also thematically recalls the *Iliad* where Agamemnon takes Briseis, Achilles' concubine, who becomes for Achilles and his comrades the symbol of his heroic honor and prestige.

[22] Michael Fishbane, Text and Texture: Close Readings of Selected Biblical Texts (New York: Schocken Books, 1979), 54.

[23] Quoted by Bruce Vawter, *On Genesis*, (note 15 above), 349.

[24] This framing is not unlike the framing in the *Odyssey,* where the hero's encounter with Poseidon and his rebirth on Scheria frame his movement from liminality to reintegration into heroic society.

[25] Fishbane, *Text and Texture*, (note 22 above), 52–3.

[26] The notion of a parallel between divine and human sovereignty in the context of a struggle against chaotic forces is also explored by the Roman poet Horace, *Odes* 3.1.

[27] Frank Cross has argued the common and ubiquitous mythic notion of the "cosmogonic battle between the creator god and Sea in West Semitic mythology." Frank M. Cross, "The Divine Warrior in Israel's Early Cult," *Biblical Motifs*, Alexander Altmann ed., (Cambridge: Harvard University Press, 1966), 16.

[28] Cf. the discussion of entropy and evolution in the final chapter of this study.

[29] I owe these observations to the perceptive remarks of Theodore H. Gaster, *The Oldest Stories in the World* (Boston: Viking Press, 1952), 67, and B. W. Anderson, *Creation*, 22.

[30] Tryggve N. D. Mettinger, *The Dethronement of Sabaoth, Studies in the Shem and Kabod Theologies*, Coniectanea Biblica, Old Testament Series 19 (Lund: C. W. K. Gleerup, 1982), 69–79

[31] Mettinger, Dethronement of Sabaoth, 72.

[32] Perhaps as a consequence of Josiah's reform, see Mettinger, *Dethronement*, 72.

[33] That Noah can be understood as the mythic hero whose efforts are responsible for the creation of order is clear from his role in building and stocking the ark. Compare Niditch, *Chaos to Cosmos*, (note 11 above), 22: "That which is special about this tale of chaos and creation is that the chaos has within it one small island of cosmogonic order, the ark." This means that Noah's building of the ark is the creative act that preserves order and thus the continuity of biological life and human social institutions.

[34] Mettinger, *Dethronement*, (note 30 above), 74.

[35] Fishbane, *Text and Texture*, (note 22 above), 12.

[36] Thus Mircea Eliade, *Cosmos and History: The Myth of the Eternal Return* (New York: Harper and Brothers, 1959), 44: "The chief differences between the man of the archaic and traditional societies and the man of the modern societies with their strong imprint of Judeo-Christianity lies in the fact that the former feels himself indissolubly

connected with the Cosmos and the cosmic rhythms, whereas the latter insists that he is connected only with History." Later in the same work, Eliade says the ancient Hebrews discovered a unique non-mythic meaning of history "as the epiphany of God" (104).

[37] Frank M. Cross, "Yahweh and the God of the Patriarchs," *HTR* 55 (1962), 253 n.123. See also Anderson, *Creation*, 53.

[38] Martin Noth expresses it thus: "the specifically Israelite reference to the exodus from Egypt now took the place of the ancient Near Eastern reference to the creation of the world." "God, King, People in the Old Testament," *JTC* 1 (1965), 39.

[39] Fishbane, *Text and Texture*, (note 22 above), 22.

Chapter VI: Epilogue

Chaos and Cosmology, the Modern View

The previous chapters of this study have endeavored to demonstrate the pervasive presence of the watery chaos mythologem in several ancient mythopoetic traditions. Believing that the chaotic forces of nature could be somehow countered by human effort, ancient storytellers sought to frame a coherent model of the universe, by which they hoped to confront crucial problems of human existence.

Modern chaos theory

Chaos has also been increasingly the focus of modern scholarship not only in the hard sciences but also, with interesting implications, in the humanities, especially in literary studies.[1] As modern thinkers have studied chaos and discovered the universal laws of chaotic systems, they have begun to change the ways in which the nature of chaos is understood. Instead of the traditional notions of void, randomness, or disorder, modern chaos theory has revealed the existence of dynamic processes in the natural world that integrate the stability and predictability of mechanistic systems with the randomness and unpredictability of chance. In the instability and randomness of chaotic events, they find process and pattern, that is, a remarkable tendency for chaos to unfold in certain predictable ways and not in others. Thus scientists have begun to understand how the evolving universe organizes itself into hierarchical structures, how chaos arises and becomes a positive force with inherent patterns and predictabilities.[2] With the discovery of new patterns of order within seemingly random congeries of natural events,[3] it has become possible to speak of "chaotic systems." Whether it be the seemingly unpredictable behavior of the stock market, the order of mathematical calculations based on random numbers, or the architectural structure of a beehive produced by *irrational* bees, all such chaotic systems seem to reveal a hidden and previously unknown orderliness.

Chaotic systems, as understood by current theory, share the following characteristics.

The Importance of Scale in the Analysis of Chaotic Systems

In contrast to the traditional scientific view that objects are independent of the scale used to measure them, modern chaos theorists have discovered that as measurement of scale decreases, there is an increase in complexity through increased dimensionality.

Perhaps the most important tool employed by chaos-theorists in this discovery has been the computer. With its ability to perform countless repetitive calculations, the computer has enabled scientists to use algorithmic calculations to formulate ways of modeling complexity and disorder to reveal underlying patterns of order in seemingly random and chaotic phenomena. These patterns of order in chaotic systems, when revealed through complex computer models and repetitive calculations, show that chaotic systems often have a rich phenomenology. They exhibit many different types of behavior, containing, for example, "windows" of ordered behavior in mainly chaotic regimes and vice versa, and transitional movement between order and chaos by various routes.

Fractal geometry (the term was coined by its discoverer, Benoit Mandelbrot) is the best visual demonstration of the phenomenon. Random numbers, repeatedly subjected to the same mathematical procedures, and then programmed to display on a computer screen, reveal increasingly complex patterns, often with exquisitely beautiful variations. This phenomenon has led to an awareness that the method of analysis can condition, indeed even *determine,* the outcome of the analysis. Hence, the intelligibility of chaotic systems varies according to the analytic methodology employed.

Therefore, when the complexity of scale is appropriately accounted for, it becomes clear that chaos, like noise, if observed with the right tools from the right position, generates meaningful forms and structures. This new way of looking at chaos involves a transformation regarding the nature of information: no longer seen as necessarily structured in linear concatenations, information now is profoundly implicated with randomness. Chaos has become a source of meaningful information, open to new and different ways of analysis and interpretation. This new species of information now makes it possible, as Nina Hall has observed, "to link everyday experiences to the laws of nature by revealing, in an aesthetically pleasing way, the subtle relationships between simplicity and complexity and between orderliness and randomness."[4]

Sensitivity to initial conditions

One of the most interesting insights of modern chaotics has been the phenomenon called "the *butterfly effect*," the term used to describe the extreme sensitivity of chaotic systems to initial conditions. As they have studied chaotic phenomena, modern scientists have noted that in a number of instances small changes lead to increasingly larger changes, indeed changes quite incommensurate with the original movements that gave them rise. This extreme sensitivity to initial conditions is one of the almost universal signatures of chaotic systems. This *butterfly effect*[5] is predicated on the mischievous notion that the effects occasioned by the movement of a butterfly's wings in South America will, when magnified over time and space, cause tornadoes in North America. The ability, then, of small fluctuations to effect large-scale changes is characteristic of chaotic phenomena such as, for example, the turbulence of fast-moving rivers, or violent weather systems, or even the wild fluctuations of the stock market.

Scientists have concluded that, unless the starting conditions can be specified with infinite precision, chaotic systems quickly become unpredictable. In contrast to systems marked by linearity, where the magnitudes of cause and effect generally correspond with a regular and predictable proportionality, the nonlinearity of chaotic systems involves large incongruities between cause and effect. Katherine Hayles refers to an article in *Scientific American* in which the authors estimate that "if an effect as small as the gravitational pull of an electron at the edge of the galaxy is neglected, the trajectories of colliding billiard balls become unpredictable *within one minute*."[6] This extreme sensitivity to small changes also means that "the behavior of systems with different initial conditions, no matter how similar, diverges exponentially as time goes on."[7]

Feedback mechanisms

Complex chaotic systems often seem to function through feedback mechanisms. Often defined as a functional iteration, a feedback loop or feedback mechanism is the process whereby the products or output of the system re-enters the same system as input. Chemical reactions, for example, may produce products, which serve as catalysts for the reaction, driving it to generate more products, which in turn become more catalyst. The resulting dynamics are instrumental in explaining how structures of greater complexity can emerge from initially simpler entities.[8] A simple example of a feedback loop might be the sound of a loudspeaker being fed back through a microphone and amplified even more to produce an unbearable squawk. A feedback mechanism can also produce stability as a thermostat does in regulating a constant temperature level.[9]

Scientists have become increasingly aware how complex physical systems often sit delicately balanced on the thin line between order and chaos. Such systems have enough stability to produce information and yet also enough changeability to mutate and evolve, creating spontaneous, self-sustaining order. Some theorists argue that this *self-organization* serves as a counterbalance to the second law of thermodynamics, according to which all of nature is subject to entropy—the inevitable winding down of all moving systems in the universe.

In classical thermodynamic theory, *entropy*[10] is the quantity of energy that gets dissipated as heat in any mechanical process or system and is, therefore, unavailable for useful work. With the passage of time, more and more energy suffers this dissipation and less and less work gets done. Thus, entropy has also come to mean an increase in the degree of disorder in a closed or isolated system such as the universe. The result of the process of entropy is thermodynamic equilibrium, when all things reach a state of unchanging stasis. Insofar as entropy is a universal principle, the universe itself, in its relentless movement toward thermodynamic equilibrium, is in a ceaseless process of "winding down." Concerning the movement from non-equilibrium to equilibrium, Peter Coveney writes:

> For the difference between equilibrium and non-equilibrium is as stark as that between a journey and its destination, or the words of this sentence and the full stop that ends it. It is only by virtue of irreversible non-equilibrium processes that a system reaches a state of equilibrium. Life itself is a non-equilibrium process: aging is irreversible. Equilibrium is reached only at death, when a decayed corpse crumbles into dust.[11]

The paradox, then, that any theory of chaotics needs to address is the reality that cosmic equilibrium has yet to be realized. The universe does not appear to be winding down, but in fact, understood as an evolving system, seems to be growing in complexity, achieving greater and greater evolutionary orderliness.

In modeling chaotic phenomena, various scholars have discovered self-replicating structures that seem to evolve by a process of natural selection. "God plays dice with the universe," Joseph Ford said, contradicting Einstein's famous aphorism, yet went on to add, "but they're loaded dice." As Gleick notes, the main goal of the physical sciences is to find out by what rules those Einsteinian dice are loaded, and how we can use them for our own ends.[12]

In these ways modern chaos theory has endeavored, with some remarkable successes, to show how it is scientifically possible to reconcile the haphazard and seemingly capricious behaviors of an immensely complex physical world with the simple and orderly underlying laws of nature,[13] and in so doing has been able to turn meaningless disorder into *significant* disorder. This reconciliation often involves the demonstration that within chaotic systems there is an underlying pattern of order and meaning, sometimes even resulting in the possibility of general and inchoate predictabilities.

Conceptual Implications of Chaos Theory

This strange, ordered disorder of chaotic systems has brought into view a *tertium quid* dwelling in a realm between order and disorder. It is a territory where one finds natural phenomena that are at the same time both deterministically ordered and unpredictable.

Implicit in the seemingly self-contradictory concept of *chaotic systems* is a revolutionary transformation regarding the nature of meaningful information: with the disappearance of clear lines of demarcation between order and disorder, randomness and predictability, in short, between *cosmos* and chaos, present day theorists have uncovered new ways of confronting the *chaos* of the natural world. As a cognitive category open to new methods of analytic interpretation, chaos is now a matrix of new kinds of information.[14]

In ways that strangely parallel developments in chaos theory, literary and cultural scholars have increasingly begun to speak of cultural fields and realms of discourse that are at once both fragmented and unified. Ours is a world of interconnectedness where instantaneous global communication is commonplace, and yet a world with local foci of specialized expertise and knowledge.[15] Steven Johnson suggests that literary critics as "theorists of complex systems" are also interested in the complexities that underlie the *chaotics* of literary composition. To mention two scholars whose work has explored points of contact between chaos theory and literary composition, Catherine Hayles and Alexander Argyros have written provocative analyses of the correspondences between the science of chaotics and the functioning of literary narratives.

Implications of Chaos Theory for Ancient Myth

I would extend the argument to include the mythic patterns that have been the concern of this study. It is possible to conceive of the Eastern Mediterranean in the second millennium BCE as a world both unified and fragmented. The fundamental mythic worldview was a cultural substratum, underlying and communicated between the great civilizations of the ancient Near East. The belief in divine powers beyond human ken (at least partially), and the assumption that the cosmos has some modicum of intelligibility formed a cultural foundation unifying these civilizations. The fragmenting and centrifugal forces were the geographic and linguistic barriers, which the civilizations of antiquity were in some measure able to overcome.

Where the ancient poets confronted the chaotic through their available conceptual tools, that is, the traditional patterns of mythic narrative and religious activity, modern students of chaos,

using the immense power of the computer and other scientific
tools of research, have also seen new and provocative patterns of
meaning. Yet the ancient poet and the modern scientist share the
same goal, that is, a fuller understanding of the world and the
ways in which it operates.

One of the fundamental suppositions of the ancient worldview
was that the physical world is, at least in part, ordered and orderly.
The rhythms of day and night, the alternation of the seasons, the
patterned and predictable movement of the stars led the ancients
to the belief that the world they experienced was an orderly
system, a *cosmos*. At the same time vagaries of weather, sundry
catastrophes of earthquake, and violent storms, demanded explanations that could somehow reconcile a world that is at once both
orderly and chaotic. Where there is cosmos, chaos is absent; when
chaos appears, cosmos vanishes. Whether these polarities are
expressed in terms of sacred and profane, liminal and societal, or
in the conceptions of hero and watery monster, they seem basic to
the pre-scientific worldview.

The gods of the universe, awesome and awful in their powers,
could and often did behave with arbitrary and capricious indifference to the human consequences of their behavior. Yet the ancient
storyteller and his protagonists clung to the belief that the gods
were endowed all the same with some sense of fair play and the
will to see justice both in the workings of the physical world and in
the realm of human affairs. What was required then, was some
method of ascertaining what motivated the gods to act as they did
and then some way of employing that knowledge to human
advantage. Too often, it seems, modern interpreters fail to appreciate the empirical dimension of ancient attempts to manipulate
divine behavior.

To cite one point of contact between ancient myth and modern chaotics, the incommensurability of cause and consequence in
the butterfly effect of modern chaotics parallels the mythic stories

that tell how the gods, incensed by a small and apparently insignificant slight, give vent to their anger with widespread human slaughter. The kidnapping, for example, of one woman leads to a great war, the death of countless thousands, and the annihilation of a once proud city. Ancient myths wrestle with the moral question how can it be fair or just for the gods to behave with such inequity.[16] The unspoken assumption is that just as there is a predictable, orderly pattern operating in the physical world, there is also a moral order whereby the punishment of the wicked is commensurate with their wrongdoing. But when the punishment exceeds the crime, when the rectifying powers of justice impose punishment far in excess of the wrong, the result is moral chaos, the ethical equivalent of cosmic entropy. The mythic worldview saw the cosmos as an organic whole, whose functioning is rational, hence fair and just. By contrast, the incommensurability of wickedness and punishment is irrational, hence chaotic. Is it out of place, then, to suggest that modern theorists of chaos begin with assumptions that are akin to those of the ancients, to wit, that in spite of the apparent randomness of many events in the cosmos, there is all the same an underlying rationality and order?

It becomes appropriate to suggest, therefore, that the underlying question that brings together the insights of the ancient mythmaker and the modern student of chaotics is whether the concepts of chaos and cosmos, random orderliness and complexity theory are appropriate tools for making sense of the world. Can it be argued that mythic patterns, indeed the very phenomenon of mythic narrative itself, can be analyzed and understood as a "system poised between orderly and chaotic states, promising to transform itself into a new, higher level of organization and at the same time prone to dissipation, turbulence, entropy"?[17]

For example, in Chapter II, the story of Gilgamesh revealed the hero as a mythic expression of liminality. Located in the interstices between chaos and order, Gilgamesh comes to represent the human confrontation with the perennial mystery of death. Both the temple prostitute, who seduces and humanizes Enkidu, and the goddess Ishtar, who attempts to wed Gilgamesh, are liminal figures and as such agents of the chaotic, who condition his movement out of and back into the ordered realm of civilization. This functional role in the movement of the *Gilgamesh Epic* calls to mind the feedback mechanisms of modern chaotics. For although they are clearly liminal, i.e. part of the chaotic realm, they are also the matrix, as it were, of greater order, new forms of social creativity, indeed of growing humanization as they interact in both negative and positive ways with the two liminal heroes of the epic. To put it somewhat differently, in their respective encounters with the liminally feminine, Gilgamesh and Enkidu grow in both liminality and sophistication, and when they subsequently move back into the realm of the non-liminal, they have acquired a better understanding of human order and creativity. As a result of this mythic feedback mechanism, their encounter with the liminal and the chaotic makes them human and humane in ways they would not have otherwise been.

So also in the chapter on Old Testament patterns of chaos, it was argued that the Babylonian Akitu festival employed ritual activity to limit the effect of chaos and at the same time to insure the continuity of cosmos. As such, I would maintain, this ritual activity functioned as a feedback mechanism, patterning itself after the chaotic and destructive (i.e. ritually deposing the reigning king) but in such a ways as to restore (through the re-enthronement ritual) equilibrium and order. This thermostat-like activity of the Akitu festival, as a cyclical celebration harmonizing the political structure with the changing seasons, echoes the way in which feedback mechanisms of current chaos-theory modulate the relationship between linearity and nonlinearity.

Modern chaos-theorists often use water imagery in their descriptions of chaos: "The science of chaos is like a river that has been fed from many streams."[18]   Similarly, the study of fluid mechanics and fluid dynamics[19] has "proved to be a useful test bed for mathematical theories modeling the transition from order to chaos."[20] To put it into other terms, just as the linear trajectories of traditional scientific explanation have given way to nonlinear turbulence as the creative matrix of scientific analysis and interpretation, so also early mythmakers turned to the mythologem of watery chaos in order to set forth an intelligible account of human endeavor in a chaotic world.

Insofar as the ancient model—the mythic conceptualizations that have informed this study—identified chaos with water, it takes on the characteristics of a primitive theory of fluid dynamics. The powers of Tehom, Scamander, Poseidon, _et al._ are encountered and defeated by the application of heroic intelligence.   In the modern model the analysis of chaos in terms of the randomness and nonlinearity of fluid systems—abetted to be sure by the computer—parallels the ancient struggle to confront, contain and even control the chaotic powers of water.[21]

Implicit in both the ancient model and the modern analysis is the fundamental question, what is chaos? Is the modern conception, like the ancient one, metaphorical in nature, or is it, because based on a mathematical model, more _scientific_? Yet, when one talks of a mathematical model, is not this also metaphorical language? I would argue, then, that both scientific description— especially as currently used by chaos-theorists—and mythic narrative share a reliance on metaphor as an integral part of their respective methodologies. Metaphors invite—indeed demand—a looking at things in new and imaginative ways. (And here I use _imaginative_ in the original etymological sense of forming _representations_ of things.) This ability to conceptualize experience in new ways is what keeps myth alive and able to address the changing circumstances of traditional societies, just as metaphorical expression helps scientists conceptualize and synthesize the results of their research.

As in the case of literary composition and other forms of cultural expression, mythic narratives also constitute complex systems of meaning, and when a particular pattern of mythic meaning manifests itself in cross-cultural contexts, i.e., in several different but connected cultures, one looks for some underlying social or cultural concern that the mythic pattern seeks to address. I would argue, then, that chaos and complexity theory are more than extended metaphors in the hands of scientists, cultural historians, or literary critics; they are, rather, highly developed methodologies for searching out the underlying patterns both in the natural world and in human culture, manifested in chaos and complexity.

In the third chapter of her book, Hayles argues that one of the central ideas in the *Education of Henry Adams* is "that chaos is conceived as capable of creation as well as destruction." To support this conclusion she quotes him:

> There is nothing unscientific in the idea that, beyond the lines of force felt by the senses, the universe may be—as it has always been—either a supersensuous chaos or a divine unity, which irresistibly attracts, and is either life or death to penetrate.[22]

The human mind has always stood in dread and awe before the immensity of the cosmos. Contemplating the mysterious, vast, and unpredictable powers of the world at large, ancient humankind saw two possibilities: either the universe was at base an irrational chaos, or the creation of unseen divine forces, which, though arbitrary and capricious, were ultimately intelligible and therefore somehow tractable, that is to say, "either a supersensuous chaos or a divine unity."

The ancient mythmaker, then, intuitively understood that there is considerable risk in misunderstanding the nature of the universe, for life and death are at stake. It is important to note that where Adams sees the two possibilities of "supersensuous chaos" or "divine unity" as mutually exclusive, Hayles wants to argue that chaos and divine unity are both possible at the same time. Although Hayles' view is problematic from the perspective of traditional logic and categories of thought, it nevertheless reflects the mythic worldview. In the ancient view, primordial chaos did not *ipso facto* negate the possibility of gods and their ongoing intervention in the workings of the world. It follows then that the modern attempt to reconcile the chaotic and the orderly in the universe is something of a return to an older, *mythic* way of conceptualizing the cosmos.

Consequently, I would argue that the mythic patterns that have been the focus of this study were not only an integral part of the ancient cultures in which they were expressed, they also give expression to the universal human experiences that lie behind all human culture. The mythic patterns revealed in ancient stories of heroic battle with the annihilating forces of wind and water imply the notion of an underlying orderliness within the randomness and unpredictability of primordial chaos. Thus, the insights of modern chaos theory contain within them some very old intuitions about the nature of reality. The old mythic view and the new science of chaotics share the conviction that the universe, in spite of its random and *chaotic* processes, is evolving and ever organizing itself into new hierarchical structures.

Just as modern science is reconsidering and reformulating its understanding of chaos, so also do myths change. This is the underlying fact of all mythic narrative. They change over time and from culture to culture as changing cultural concerns motivate the mythic storytellers. These changes, notwithstanding their apparently random and seemingly irrational nature, all the same reflect an underlying consistency of meaning. Just as feedback mechanisms create greater complexity in chaotic systems, myths in general as well as specific mythologems evolve into narratives expressing deeper levels of human awareness; similarly, they may also suffer a kind of entropy, in which the living, dynamic meaning not only becomes ossified into meaningless ritual, but more importantly fails to excite the imagination of the human community.

Chaos Theory and Ancient Society

Not only do myths change, they also serve in their own right as agents of social and cultural change. In other words, any analysis of myth and ritual, in order truly to grasp their inherent power, must address the question of how the power of mythic narrative can and does become a catalyst for creative change in the social and cultural realms. Here too the feedback mechanism of chaos theory offers a relevant parallel.

On another level, chaos theory can also clarify the relation between mythic and ritual modes of encountering reality. The point of contact between myth and ritual is the inherent patterning involved in each of these approaches toward the understanding and manipulation of the external world. Understanding or *seeing* the patterns, even on a subrational or intuitive level, the ancient thinker was able both to appreciate the nuanced implication of the myth and to participate in the corresponding ritual. This experience involved the interpenetration of randomness and order. It was and is an esthetic experience in that the mythic narrator no less than his audience intuitively experienced the *beauty* of the story in both the telling and the ritual recreation. Modern chaos theory has revealed its ability to demonstrate "the unpredictable and discontinuous emergence of higher levels of systemic complexity."[23] When such complexities are given visual expression e.g. through the computer generated images of fractal geometry, the esthetic dimension of modern chaotics reveals itself in strikingly beautiful pictures.[24]

Similarly, both myth and ritual can be seen as self-similar systems, revealing similar patterns of organization at different levels of meaning, and thus can be described as nonlinear, dynamic systems able to create, on a number of different cognitive levels, more sublime levels of intelligibility than previously existed.

Liminality and Chaos Theory

It is perhaps a truism to suggest that the myths and rituals of the ancient world also reflect patterns of meaning amid the social disorder of ancient societies. These myths and rituals inevitably served the role of conceptualizing and making intelligible the complex hierarchies common to every human society. However, they also served as the mechanism by which those hierarchies were modified, developed, and raised to yet greater levels of complexity.

Argyros argues that primitive rituals, by creating a state of liminality, function as tools of social evolution akin to genetic engineering.[25] Liminality, located in the interstices of society is, as it were, the social laboratory in which the foundations of a culture are rehearsed, tested, tuned, enforced, and altered. To draw the parallel to chaos theory, liminality duplicates the pattern of chaotic systems, by which new structures evolve out of the interplay between randomness and order. The movement from social order to the disorder of liminality and back to social order is akin to the chaotic disruption occurring in natural processes, by which random events, governed by feedback loops of larger and larger scales, produce new patterns of order. Thus, liminality, seen as an ancient form of self-organization is a kind of cultural engineering. Ancient societies, in obedience to the authority of timeless rituals, use liminal experiences not only to strengthen social bonds, but also to create new and putatively better social structures.

Ritual liminality is at the core an educative process, a way of passing on stable cultural values to the next generation. It stands to reason that these values need to be tested by liminal experience, if the next generation is to accept and use them as its own. Liminality, then, is a means of ensuring that important social values do not suffer cultural entropy, i.e., devolution into meaninglessness.[26]

Much the same argument can be advanced regarding the meaning of the ancient myths. It often happens that modern readers find a mythic tale to be confused, random, unstructured, and meaningless. They need some epistemological key, some interpretive method, by which to unlock the patterns of meaning inherent in the mythic confusion. Where modern chaos theorists have been able to make use of the vast computational powers of the computer to reveal the patterns inherent in chaotic systems, I have endeavored to use the analytic tools discussed in the first chapter. Although they lack the computational precision of the computer, these tools have provided the means to analyze the patterns and structures of ancient mythic narratives.

By way of example, let me refer to the earlier discussion of the *Odyssey,* where I argued that stories of post-war homecomings involve movement from the chaos of war to the order and tranquility of peaceful home life. The story of the *Odyssey* not only limns the hero's journey from chaos to order; its mythic pattern also suggests a return from liminality in the form of a symbolic rebirth and apotheosis. As a movement from death to life, from chaos to order, it parallels the phenomenon in chaotic theory whereby in place of expected entropy, there are processes of self-organization (not well understood, to be sure) that lead to greater order, clarity and structure in the physical world. This paradoxical movement parallels the ambiguous nature of Odysseus' rebirth and apotheosis in the episodes of his encounter with Calypso and Ino-Leucothea. Had Odysseus chosen immortality by remaining with Calypso, it would have been an immortality of complete emancipation from the chaotic, the static unchanging condition of spiritual and mental equilibrium with no possibility of human growth or development. Such immortality is nothing other than the immutable stasis of death itself, in short, the mythic equivalent of *entropy* and cosmic equilibrium. Thus, the mythic pattern implicit in Odysseus' choice of life over immortality along with the mental ideology underlying it anticipates modern chaotics and the notion of cosmic *rebirth* through the processes of entropy-reversing self-organization.

Conclusions: The Epistemological Issue

Modern chaos theory has revealed a universe that is communicative across many of its hierarchical levels, dynamic in its processes of growth and evolution, and increasingly open to the disclosure of its delicate balance between predictability and randomness, in short, between order and chaos. This dynamic model of the universe as a chaotic system, neither random nor deterministic, has much in common with the mythic worldview of the ancient storytellers, who similarly saw the cosmos infused with chaotic elements yet also working in a predictable and orderly fashion. The gods and the powers they represent are both predictable and capricious, in other words, neither random nor deterministic. But where does that leave us as we endeavor to find something concrete and unchangeable on which to fix our cosmic understanding of the world?

Stephen Hawking, in his 1988 book, *A Brief History of Time*, argues that the universe "should be knowable" by human beings. Rejecting the possibility that its existence is merely "a lucky chance," Hawking states that such a theory of lucky chance is "the counsel of despair, a negation of all our hopes of understanding the underlying order of the universe."[27] In answer to Hawking's desire that there be some principle of intelligibility to account for the universe's order, Hayles observes:

> Such remarks lead one to believe that Hawking's dissatisfaction with big-bang cosmologies is commingled with

> questions about God, and that the range of possible solu-
> tions is constrained by the kind of God he can accept—
> namely, a God who agrees in advance to make the uni-
> verse understandable at every point by human beings.[28]

My difficulty with Hayles' argument lies in the rigid and absolute dichotomy it sets up: the universe is either intelligible or
unintelligible; there seems no third possibility. Yet even the
briefest of historical reflection would suggest that our twentieth
century understanding of the cosmos is vastly more sophisticated
than that of even the most advanced ancient Babylonian or Greek.
That we have learned something in five thousand years of inquiry
would argue for some modicum of intelligibility inhering in the
cosmos. At the same time, Hayles is right to question Hawking's
desire for "God who agrees in advance to make the universe
understandable at every point by human beings." Were there such
a universe, indeed were we such human beings as to understand
the universe at every point, God would be superfluous; for we
would then be omniscient and omnipotent—gods in our own right.
The fact is that human understanding is imperfect—we see in a
mirror dimly. This does not of course keep us from formulating
theories about the ways in which the world works, but such
theories will always be inchoate at best, erroneous at worst; for, as
the ancient mythic imagination clearly saw, the intelligibility of the
cosmos is indistinct and partial.

Having said all that, I would still argue the importance of rec-
ognizing that such incomplete visions still have the power to
persuade, to give expression to the needs and aspirations of
specific communities. Hayles argues that these visions produce
and are produced by a cultural matrix:

> But visions take hold and spread because they speak to
> something in the cultural moment. They signify more
> than the research can demonstrate; and it is this excess
> signification that produces and is produced by the cul-
> tural matrix. Prigogine's vision is of a universe rich in

> productive disorder, from which self-organizing struc-
> tures spontaneously arise and stabilize themselves... The
> vision sees nothingness and somethingness joined in a
> complex dance, in which vacuums are never truly empty
> and gaps are never merely ruptures.[29]

Hence, in offering a structured account of the cosmos, mythic narrative is not necessarily in error. In one way or another, it is in touch with the essential nature of the universe and its order. Just as modern chaos theorists are discovering patterns of order in the natural world that have always been there, but until recently were beyond our cognitive reach, so also the ancient myths may very well have apprehended something profoundly true: the universe is open, at least in part, to human reason and understanding. Not only do its powers and movements evolve from lower to higher levels, but also its randomness and irrationalities, when rightly understood, can be manipulated and controlled for human good.

The patterns of mythic narrative correspond in usually discernible ways to important features of the human environment, especially when the patterns involve dynamic, causal relationships. This seems particularly true of social environments. The interplay between meaningful pattern and random disorder is often expressed in the mythic narrative through metaphors, which preserve with greater or lesser clarity the underlying causal relationship. Insofar as the mythic narrative is an attempt to account for the ways in which the world works, to frame as it were a universalizing hypothesis about causes and effects, the mythic narrator is a student of chaotic systems. He attempts to give expression to the patterns and structures that lie hidden in the randomness and *chaos* of the world around him. Cognitively he is making comparisons between the models (or patterns) he has formulated in his own mind and other external models (coming from his senses or some other external source). Given the pervasive presence and long traditions of mythic thought in the Near East, the subtle interconnection of transcultural contacts, and the sophistication of Mediterranean myth, the resulting narratives are noteworthy for the complexity of their structures and conceptualizations.

In other words, the mythologem and the mythic accounts in which it is embedded have come about as a result of the ancient mythmakers' attempt to explain the order they observed, even when it seemed most chaotic. This cognitive enterprise focused on the natural world no less than the social and psychological, and succeeded precisely to the extent that it made its explanations intelligible and persuasive to its hearers. Less persuasive narratives may be said to have failed either by want of insight, that is, a less than adequate grasp of the systemic, patterned nature of the cogitanda, or by reason of the genuinely chaotic nature of the things being explained. Even so, the essential activity is the attempt to set forth a meaningful narrative of the universe's order and chaos. This study has attempted to explore the literary, mythic, ritualistic, social, and psychological implications of that ancient mythic story.

Insofar as the ancient explanations themselves are the products of the intersection of order and chaos in the mental processes of the ancient mythmakers, that is to say, their speculations both rational and intuitive, there remains a remarkable parallelism between the structure of their myths and the dynamic, evolutionary processes modern chaos theory has discovered. Because the intellectual confrontation with the chaotic is an old mythic activity, and because thinking about chaos is a paradigmatic way of thinking about cosmic questions[30] as they pertain to human values and the place of human beings in the universe, I would argue that the old mythic narratives share many of the assumptions and perspectives of modern chaos theory.

If there is then, as I argue, a correspondence between the new understanding of the universe through the science of chaotics and the patterns of ancient mythic thought, we have the means at hand to appreciate how ancient speculations about watery chaos antici-pate current theories of how the world functions as a chaotic system.   Ancient myths about watery chaos consist of narrative structures, articulated in and through language and linguistic patterns.   They arise and function within specific social and political contexts, changing and evolving through time, and yet retaining a consistent ability to speak to the human condition. Thus they give expression to all those hopes, aspirations, and fears that have defined what it means to be human, from the first stirrings of civilization in ancient Sumer up to the current efforts of scientists and cosmologists to understand the nature of chaos.

Notes to Epilogue

1 See e.g. N. Katherine Hayles, Chaos Bound: Orderly Disorder in Contemporary Literature and Science (Ithaca: Cornell University Press, 1990), and Alexander J. Argyros, A Blessed Rage for Order: Deconstruction, Evolution, and Chaos (Ann Arbor: University of Michigan Press, 1991).

2 Hayles, Chaos Bound, 3.

3 Argyros, A Blessed Rage for Order, 239.

4 Nina Hall, Exploring Chaos: A Guide to the New Science of Disorder (New York: W.W. Norton, 1991), 7.

5 This term was introduced by James Gleick, *Chaos: Making a New Science,* 1987, to characterize how small, apparently insignificant events, trigger a chain of events that lead to large consequences: the flapping of a butterfly's wings trigger a tornado on the other side of the world.

6 Hayles *op. cit.* (note 1 above), 13, Crutchfield, Farmer, Packard, and Shaw, *Scientific American,* 1986.

7 Peter Coveney, "Chaos, entropy, etc." in Hall, *op. cit.* (note 4 above), 210.

8 I am indebted to Hayles, *op. cit.* (note 1 above), pp. 11–14 for a useful summary of these characteristics of chaotic systems.

9 Gleick, *op. cit.* (note 5 above), 61.

10 The term *entropy* was first used by the German physicist Rudolf Clausius in the nineteenth century.

11 In Hall, *op. cit.* (note 4 above), 205.

12 Gleick, *op. cit.* (note 5 above), 314.

13 Paul Davies in Hall, *op. cit.* (note 4 above), 220.

14 Cf. Bruce Clarke, "Resistance in Theory and the Physics of the Text," *New Orleans Review* (Loyola University, New Orleans, LA., vol. 18 [1991]), 87.

15 Cf. Hayles again, *op. cit.* (note 1 above), 4.

[16] Cf. the poet's anguished cry at the beginning of Vergil's *Aeneid: Tantaene animis caelestibus irae?*

[17] Steven Johnson, "Strange Attraction," *Lingua Franca*, March/April 1996, 43.

[18] Ian Percival, *Chaos: A Science for the Real World,* in Hall, *op. cit.* (note 4 above), 16.

[19] In fluid dynamics chaos goes under the name of turbulence. Traditional physics finds fluids to be particularly recalcitrant, unpredictable, and unstable. Cf. Clark, *op. cit.* (note 14 above), p91.

[20] Tom Mullin, "Turbulent Times for Fluids," in Hall, *op. cit.* (note 4 above), 59.

[21] I would like to draw a parallel between the concept of a universal flood, which returns the universe to primordial conditions, and the phenomenon chaos theorists call entropy, i.e. the winding down, the process of dissipation, which tends to restore the universe to the undifferentiated state that existed before creation. However, unlike the Babylonian response in the Akitu festival, there is no evidence that the ancient Israelites endeavored to use ritual to address the crisis occasioned by the flood. Perhaps the reason was that they understood the flood story in non-ritual terms, that is to say, as a unique and solitary non-recurring event. God's promise never again to destroy the world in such a way points in that direction. Instead, with both the flood story and the Exodus event their understanding of history and historical processes changed. No longer cyclical, history for them was linear, starting with the "let there by light" of monotheistic deity; they saw history moving in a straight line into eternity.

[22] Hayles, *op. cit.* (note 1 above) 89.

[23] Argyros, *op. cit.* (note 1 above), 287.

[24] Cf. Ian Stewart's chapter, "Portraits of Chaos," in Hall, *op. cit.* (note 4 above), pp. 44-58.

[25] Argyros, *op. cit.* (note 1 above), 284.

[26] Cf. Argyros, *ibid.*

[27] Stephen Hawking, A Brief History of Time: From the Big Bang to Black Holes (New York, 1988), 133.

184 The Hero and the Sea

[28] Hayles, *op. cit.* (note 1 above), 113.

[29] Hayles, *op. cit.* (note 1 above), 114.

[30] Cf. the chapter "Chaos and Culture: Deep Assumptions of the New Paradigm," in Hayles, *op. cit.* (note 1 above).

※
Bibliography

Ahl, Frederick, and Hanna M. Roisman. *The Odyssey Re-formed* Ithaca: Cornell University Press, 1996.

Altmann, Alexander, ed. *Biblical Motifs*. Cambridge: Harvard University Press, 1966.

Anderson, B. W. *Creation Versus Chaos, The Reinterpretation of Mythical Symbolism in the Bible*. New York: Association Press, 1967.

Argyros, Alexander J. *A Blessed Rage for Order: Deconstruction, Evolution, and Chaos*. Ann Arbor: University of Michigan Press, 1991.

Austin, Norman. *Archery at the Dark of the Moon: Poetic Problems in Homer's Odyssey*. Berkeley: University of California Press, 1975.

Aycock, W. M. and T. M. Klein, *Classical Mythology in Twentieth-Century Thought and Literature*. Lubbock, Texas: Texas Tech Press, 1978.

Barbour, Ian G. *Myths, Models, and Paradigms: A Comparative Study in Science and Religion*. New York: Harper & Row, 1974.

Bannert, Herbert. "Zur Vogelgestalt der Götter bei Homer." *Wiener Studien*, 91 (1978): 29–42.

Bergren, Ann L. T. "Odyssean Temporality: Many (Re)turns." *In Approaches to Homer*, edition C. A. Rubino & C. W. Shelmerdine. Austin: University of Texas Press, 1983.

Bergren, Ann L. T. "Allegorizing Winged Words: Similes and Symbolization in Odyssey V." *Classical World* 74 (October 1980): 109–123.

Bernal, Martin. *Black Athena: the Afroasiatic Roots of Classical Civilization.* Vol. I. New Brunswick, NJ: Rutgers University Press, 1987.

Beye, Charles. *The Iliad, Odyssey, and Epic Tradition.* London: Macmillan, 1968.

Burkert, Walter. *Homo Necans: The Anthropology of Ancient Greek Sacrificial Ritual and Myth.* Berkeley, CA: University of California Press, 1983.

_____. *Structure and History in Greek Mythology and Ritual.* Berkeley, CA: University of California Press, 1979.

Campbell, Joseph. *The Hero with a Thousand Faces.* Princeton, NJ: Princeton University Press, 1968.

Clarke, Bruce. "Resistance in Theory and the Physics of the Text," *New Orleans Review.* (Loyola University, New Orleans, LA., vol. 18 (1991).

Clay, Jenny Strauss. *The Wrath of Athena: Gods and Man in the Odyssey.* Princeton: Princeton University Press, 1983.

Cohn, Robert L. *The Shape of Sacred Space: Four Biblical Studies.* Chico, CA: Scholars Press, 1981.

Cross, Frank M. "The Divine Warrior in Israel's Early Cult." In *Biblical Motifs,* edited by Alexander Altmann ed. Cambridge: Harvard University, 1966.

Cross, Frank M. "Yahweh and the God of the Patriarchs." *HTR* 55 (1962).

Dalley, Stephanie. *Myths from Mesopotamia: Creation, The Flood, Gilgamesh and Others.* Oxford: Oxford University Press, 1989.

Dimock, George. "The Name of Odysseus." *The Hudson Review* IX, no. 1 (Spring 1956): 52–70.

Dimock, George. *The Unity of the Odyssey.* Amherst, MA: The University of Massachusetts Press, 1989.

Edmunds, Lowell, ed. *Approaches to Greek Myth*. Baltimore: Johns Hopkins University Press, 1990.

Eliade, Mircea. *Cosmos and History: The Myth of the Eternal Return*. Translated by Willard Trask. New York: Harper and Brothers, 1954.

____. *Images and Symbols: Studies in Religious Symbolism*. Tanslated by Philip Mairet. New York: Sheed and Ward, 1969.

____. *Myth and Reality*. Tanslated by Willard Trask, New York: Harper & Row, 1963.

____. "Mythologies of Death: An Introduction." In *Religious Encounters with Death*, edited by Frank E. Reynolds and Earle H. Waugh. University Park, PA: Pennsylvania State University Press, 1977.

____. *Rites and Symbols of Initiation: the Mysteries of Birth and Rebirth*. Translated by Willard Trask. New York: Harper & Row, 1958.

Farnell, L. R. "Ino-Leucothea." *JHS* XXXVI (1916) 36–44.

Fishbane, Michael. *Text and Texture: Close Readings of Selected Biblical Texts*. New York: Schocken Books, 1979.

Fontenrose, Joseph. *Orion: The Myth of the Hunter and the Huntress*. Berkeley: University of California Press, 1981.

____. *Python, A Study of Delphic Myth and its Origins*. New York: Biblo & Tannen, 1974.

____. "The Sorrows of Ino and of Procne." *TAPA* 79 (1948), 125–167.

____. "White Goddess and Syrian Goddess." *University of California Publications in Semitic Philology*, Vol. 11, 125–148.

Frame, Douglas. *The Myth of Return in Early Greek Epic*. New Haven: Yale University Press, 1978.

Galinsky, Karl. *The Heracles Theme: the Adaptations of the Hero in Literature from Homer to the Twentieth Century.* Totowa, NJ: Rowman and Littlefield, 1972.

Gardner, John, and John Maier. *Gilgamesh.* New York: Alfred A. Knopf, 1984.

Garelli, P. *Gilgames et sa légende: Études recueillies par Paul Garelli à l'occasion de la VIIe Rencontre Assyriologique Internationale.* Paris: Librairie C. Klincksieck, 1960.

Gaster, Theodor H. *The Oldest Stories in the World.* Boston: Vicking Press, 1952.

Gleick, James. *Chaos: Making a New Science.* New York: Viking, 1987.

Gordon, R. L., ed. *Myth, Religion, Society: Structuralist Essays.* New York: Cambridge University Press, 1981.

Gottwald, Norman K., *The Hebrew Bible: A Socio-Literary Introduction.* Philadelphia: Fortress Press, 1985.

Gresseth, Gerald K. "The Gilgamesh Epic and Homer." *Classical Journal* 70 (1975): 1–18.

Günkel, Hermann. *Schöpfung und Chaos in Urzeit und Endzeit.* Göttingen: Vandenhoeck und Ruprecht, 1895.

Hall, Nina, ed. *Exploring Chaos: A Guide to the New Science of Disorder.* New York: W.W. Norton, 1991.

Hawking, Stephen W. *A Brief History of Time: From the Big Bang to Black Holes.* New York: Bantam Books, 1988.

Hayles, N. Katherine. *Chaos Bound: Orderly Disorder in Contemporary Literature and Science.* Ithaca: Cornell University Press, 1990.

Heidel, Alexander. *The Gilgamesh Epic and Old Testament Parallels.* Chicago: University of Chicago Press, 1963.

Heubeck, Alfred, Stephanie West, and J. B. Hainsworth. *A Commentary on Homer's Odyssey, Volume I: Introduction and Books I–VIII.* Oxford: Clarendon Press, 1988.

Holtsmark, Erling B. "Spiritual Rebirth of the Hero: Odyssey 5." *Classical Journal* 61 (February, 1966) 206–210.

Honko, Lauri. "Theories Concerning the Ritual Process: An Orientation." In *Science of Religion, Studies in Methodology: Proceedings of the Study Conference of the International Association for the History of Religions,* edited by Lauri Honko. The Hague: Mouton Publishers, 1979.

Huxley, George Leonard. *Greek epic poetry from Eumelos to Panyassis.* Cambridge: Harvard University Press, 1969.

Jackson, Danny P., translator. *The Epic of Gilgamesh.* Wauconda, Illinois: Bolchazy-Carducci, 1992.

Jacobsen, Thorkild. "The Battle between Marduk and Ti'amat." *Journal of the American Oriental Society* 88 (1968).

_____. *The Harps That Once—Sumerian Poetry in Translation.* New Haven: Yale University Press, 1987.

Johnson, Steven. "Strange Attraction." *Lingua Franca* March–April (1996).

Kaiser, Otto. *Die mythische Bedeutung des Meeres in Äegypten, Ugarit, und Israel.* Berlin: Töpelmann, 1962.

Kardulias, Dianna Rhyan. "Odysseus in Ino's Veil: Feminine Headdress and the Hero in *Odyssey* 5." *TAPA* 131 (2001) 23–51.

Kerényi, Karl. *Goddesses of Sun and Moon.* Irving, Texas: Spring Publications, 1979.

Kirk, G. S. *Myth, its Meaning and Functions in Ancient and other Cultures.* Sather Classical Lectures, vol. 40. Berkeley: University of California Press, 1970.

Kluckhohn, Clyde. *Anthropology and the Classics.* Providence, Rhode Island: Brown University Press, 1961.

Kluckhohn, Clyde. "Myths and Rituals: A General Theory." Originally published in *Harvard Theological Review* 35 (1942, pp. 45–79); republished in Robert A. Segal, *The Myth and Ritual Theory, An Anthology,* 1998. Oxford: Blackwell Publishers, 1998, pp. 313–34.

Kramer, Samuel Noah. "The Epic of Gilgamesh and Its Sumerian Sources." *Journal of the American Oriental Society* 54 (1944).

_____. "Gilgamesh and the Land of the Living," *Journal of Cuneiform Studies* 1 (1947).

Kramer, Samuel Noah, and Diane Wolkstein. *Inanna, Queen of Heaven and Earth: Her Stories and Hymns from Sumer.* New York: Harper & Row, 1983.

Lambert, W. G., and A. R. Millard. *Atrahasis, the Babylonian Story of the Flood, with the Sumerian Flood Story, by M. Civil.* London: Oxford University Press, 1969.

Lloyd-Jones, Hugh. *The Justice of Zeus.* 2nd ed. Berkeley: University of California Press, 1983.

Lord, Albert B. *The Singer of Tales.* Cambridge: Harvard University, 1964.

Lord, Mary Louise. "Withdrawal and Return: An Epic Story Pattern in the Homeric Hymn to Demeter and in the Homeric Poems." *Classical Journal* 62 (1967), 242–48.

Lorenz, Edward N. *The Essence of Chaos.* Seattle: University of Washington Press, 1993.

Louden, Bruce. *The Odyssey, Structure, Narration, and Meaning.* Baltimore: Johns Hopkins University Press, 1999.

Malinowski, Bronislaw. *Myth in Primitive Psychology.* New York: Norton & Co., 1926.

Mettinger, Tryggve N. D. *The Dethronement of Sabaoth. Studies in the Shem and Kabod Theologies.* Coniectanea Biblica, Old Testament Series 19, Lund: C. W. K. Gleerup, 1982.

Mills, D. H. "Tibullus and Phaeacia, a Reinterpretation of I.3." *The Classical Journal*, 69 (1974), 226–233.

_____. "Odysseus and Polyphemus: Two Homeric Similes Reconsidered." *The Classical Outlook* 58 (May–June 1981).

_____. "Sacred Space in Vergil's *Aeneid*." *Vergilius* 29 (1983).

Moran, W. L. "Atrahasis: The Babylonian Story of the Flood." *Biblica* 52 (1971).

Nagler, Michael. *Spontaneity and Tradition: A Study in the Oral Art of Homer*. Berkeley: University of California, 1974.

Nagy, Gregory. *The Best of the Achaeans: Concepts of the Hero in Archaic Greek Poetry*. Baltimore: John Hopkins University Press, 1979.

Niditch, Susan. *Chaos to Cosmos: Studies in Biblical Patterns of Creation*. Chico, California: Scholars Press, 1985.

Noth, Martin. "God, King, People in the Old Testament." *JTC* 1 (1965).

Oppenheim, Leo A. *Ancient Mesopotamia: Portrait of a Dead Civilization*. Chicago: University of Chicago Press, 1977.

Penglase, Charles. *Greek Myths and Mesopotamia: Parallels and Influence in the Homeric Hymns and Hesiod*. New York: Routledge, 1994.

Prigogine, Ilya. *Order Out of Chaos: Man's New Dialogue with Nature*. Boulder, Colorado: New Science Library, 1984

Pritchard, James Bennett. *Ancient Near Eastern Texts Relating to the Old Testament (ANET)*. 3rd ed. Princeton NJ: Princeton University Press, 1969.

Propp, William Henry. *Water in the Wilderness: A Biblical Motif and Its Mythological Background*. Atlanta GA: Scholars Press, 1987.

Pucci, Pietro. *Odysseus Polutropos: Intertextual Readings in the Odyssey and The Iliad.* Ithaca: Cornell University Press, 1987.

Raven, O. E. "The Passage on Gilgamesh and the Wives of Uruk." *Bibliotheca Orientalis* 10 (1953).

Redfield, James M. *Nature and Culture in the Iliad: The Tragedy of Hector.* Expanded ed. Durham: Duke University Press, 1994.

Reece, Steve. *The Stranger's Welcome: Oral Theory and the Aesthetics of the Homeric Hospitality Scene.* Ann Arbor: University of Michigan Press, 1993.

Reynolds, Frank E., and Earle H. Waugh. *Religious Encounters with Death: Insights from the History and Anthropology of Religions.* University Park PA: Pennsylvania State University Press, 1977.

Sandars, N. K. *The Epic of Gilgamesh.* New York: Penguin Books, 1972.

Schein, S. L. *The Mortal Hero: An Introduction to Homer's Iliad.* Berkeley CA, 1984.

Schmitt, A. *Selbstständigkeit und Abhängigkeit menschlichen Handels bei Homer: Hermeneutische Untersuchungen zur Psychologie Homers.* Akademie der Wissenschaften und der Literatur, Mainz: Abhandlungen der geistes und sozialwissenschaftlichen Klasse, Abh. 5. Stuttgart, 1990.

Schwabl, H. "Zur Selbständigkeit des Menschen bei Homer." *Wiener Studien* 67 (1954): 46–64.

Segal, Charles. "The Phaeacians and the Symbolism of Odysseus' Return." *Arion* 1 (1962): 17–63

Segal, Charles. "Transition and Ritual in Odysseus' Return." *La Parola Del Passato* 22 (1967): 321–342.

Segal, Robert A., ed. *Ritual and Myth: Robertson Smith, Frazer, Hooke, and Harrison.* New York: Garland, 1996

Segal, Robert A. ed. *The Myth and Ritual Theory, An Anthology.* Oxford: Blackwells, 1998.

Shay, Jonathan. *Achilles in Vietnam: Combat Trauma and the Undoing of Character.* New York: Atheneum, 1994.

Steiner, George, and Robert Fagles. *Homer: A Collection of Critical Essays.* Englewood Cliffs, NJ: Prentice Hall, 1962.

Thompson, William Irwin. *The Time Falling Bodies Take to Light: Mythology, Sexuality and the Origins of Culture.* New York: St. Martin's Press, 1981.

Tigay, J. H. *The Evolution of the Gilgamesh Epic.* Philadelphia: University of Pennsylvania Press, 1982.

Tillich, Paul. "The Religious Symbol." *Daedalus* (1958).

Turner, Victor. "Death and the Dead in the Pilgrimage Process," in *Religious Encounters with Death.* Edited by Reynolds and Waugh. University Park PA: Pennsylvania State University Press, 1977, 24–39.

Turner, Victor. *The Ritual Process, Structure and Anti-Structure.* Chicago: Aldine Publishing Company, 1969.

Van Buren, E. D. "The Sacred Marriage in Early Times in Mesopotamia." *Orientalia* 13 (1944).

Van Gennep, Arnold. *Les Rites de Passage: Étude systématique des rites de la Porte et du seuil, de l'hospitalité, de l'adoption, de la Grossesse et de l'accouchement, de la naissance, de L'enfance, de la puberté, de l'initiation, de l'ordination, Du couronnement des fiançailles et du mariage, des Funérailles, des saisons, etc.* 1909. Reprint, New York: Johnson Reprint Corporation, 1969.

Van Gennep, Arnold. *The Rites of Passage.* Translated by Monika Vizedom and Gabrielle Caffee, London: Routledge & Paul, 1960.

Van Nortwick, Thomas. *Somewhere I Have Never Travelled: the Second Self and the Hero's Journey in Ancient Epic.* New York: Oxford University Press, 1992.

Vawter, Bruce. *On Genesis: A New Reading.* Garden City, NY: Doubleday, 1977.

Vickery, John B. *Myth and Literature.* Lincoln NE, 1969.

____. *Myths and Texts: Strategies of Incorporation and Displacement.* Baton Rouge, LA: Louisiana State University Press, 1983.

Vidal-Naquet, P. *The Black Hunter: Forms of Thought and Forms of Society in the Greek World.* Baltimore, 1986.

Vizedom, Monica. *Rites and Relationships: Rites of Passage and Contemporary Anthropology.* Beverly Hills, CA: Sage Publications, 1976.

Von Rad, Gerhard. *Genesis: A Commentary.* Old Testament Library Old Testament Theology. Philadelphia: Westminster Press, 1961.

Webster, T. B. L. *From Mycenae to Homer.* London, 1958.

Westermann, Claus. *Genesis 1–11: A Commentary.* Trans. by John J. Scullion. Minneapolis: Augsburg Publishing House, 1984.

Whitman, Cedric. *The Heroic Paradox, Essays on Homer, Sophocles, and Aristophanes.* Ithaca, NY: Cornell University Press, 1982.

____. *Homer and the Heroic Tradition.* Cambridge: Harvard University Press, 1958.

Wolff, Hope N. "Gilgamesh, Enkidu, and the Heroic Life." *Journal of the American Oriental Society* 89 (1969).

※
Index